What Would Jesus Pair?

Celebrating God's gift of food and wine

PAMELA HILL SHARP

Copyright © 2023 by Pamela Hill Sharp
First Paperback Edition

All rights reserved. No part of this publication may be reproduced, distributed, or transmitted in any form or by any means, including photocopying, recording, or other electronic or mechanical methods, without the prior written permission of the publisher, except in the case of brief quotations embodied in critical reviews and certain other noncommercial uses permitted by copyright law. For permission requests, write to the publisher, addressed "Attention: Permissions Coordinator," at the address below.

Unless otherwise indicated, Scripture references are taken from The Holy Bible, English Standard Version. ESV® Text Edition: 2016. Copyright © 2001 by Crossway Bibles, a publishing ministry of Good News Publishers.

Some names, businesses, places, events, locales, incidents, and identifying details inside this book have been changed to protect the privacy of individuals.

Published by Freiling Agency, LLC.

P.O. Box 1264
Warrenton, VA 20188

www.FreilingAgency.com

PB ISBN: 979-8-9888007-2-9
eBook ISBN: 979-8-9888007-3-6

Printed in the United States of America

Dedication

To my husband, Rob, for encouraging me to live out my dreams, and not only in the world of wine, but in all of life's adventures.

To my sons, Spencer and Alec, for continually cheering me on and always showing your unwavering love for me. I love you more.

Table of Contents

Acknowledgments ix
Introduction xiii
Prologue xix

Section I

1 The Real Jesus 3
2 The Gift of Wine 11
3 Bread of Heaven 21
4 Bread of Life 33
5 Feasts and Celebrations 45
6 Blessed Generations 55

Section II

7   A Garden of Eden 71
8   Bartered for a Bowl of Stew 81
9   Saint Peter's Fish 89
10 A Wedding At Cana 97
11 Harvest of Plenty 107
12 I Am the Vine 115

Section III

13 A Land of Milk and Honey 127

Section IV

14 A Glance At The Ancient World of Wine 149
15 Dinner with Jesus 163
16 What Would Jesus Drink? 177

Section V

17	The Lord's Supper in Light of Passover	193
18	Observance of the Passover Seder	205
19	A Passover Meal and Menu	213
20	A Short Family Messianic Haggadah	219
21	Conclusion	237

Section VI

22	The Art of Pairing	243
23	The Recipes	255

BREADS AND BREAKFAST 255
    Solomon's Flat Bread (Crackers) 255
    Ezekiel's Bread 256
    Easy Flatbread (No Yeast) 258
    Biblical Barley Cakes (Biscuits) 260
    Creamy Barley Breakfast Porridge 261

APPETIZERS / CHARCUTERIE 263
    Spiced Wine 263
    Classic Marinated Olives 264
    Olive Tapenade 265
    Hummus 266
    Dolmas (Stuffed Grape Leaves) 267
    Grape and Prosciutto Crostini 269
    Spiced Pear and Pomegranate Crostini 270
    Brie en Croûte with Thyme and
    Fig Jam 271
    Goat Cheese Stuffed Dates 273
    Pomegranate Relish 274
    Gefilte Fish Appetizer (Doctored from
    a jar) 275

Table of Contents

SOUPS 277
    Mimi's Lentil Soup 277
    Classic Chicken Matzah Ball Soup........... 279

SALADS AND SIDES 282
    Vanilla Fig Dressing 282
    Egyptian Barley Salad with Pomegranate Vinaigrette 282
    Classic Mediterranean Tabbouleh Salad 284
    Roasted Beet Salad with Lentils and Goat Cheese 286
    Brown Butter Lentil and Sweet Potato Salad 288
    Chickpea Pomegranate Salad................. 290
    Charoset Salad 290
    Cantaloupe Melon Salad with Cucumber and Feta 291
    Barley Roasted Mediterranean Vegetables 292
    Mediterranean Roasted Eggplant............ 294
    Fruited Israeli Couscous 296
    Apple Matzah Kugel 298

FISH, POULTRY, AND MEAT 300
    Whole Baked St. Peter's Fish................. 300
    Lemon Cream Sauce.......................... 302
    Green Goddess Sauce 303
    Greek Ladolemono Sauce.................... 304
    Romesco Sauce 304
    Mediterranean Fish Stew 305
    Mediterranean Spiced Game Hens.......... 307
    Roasted Chicken with Lemon and Thyme 309
    Creamy Pheasant Breasts 310

Passover Beef Brisket 312
Lamb with Figs and Red Wine 314

DESSERTS.. 316
Red Wine Poached Pears 316
Honey Almond Cake 317
Flourless Chocolate Cake 319
Song of Songs Nut Cakes 321

24   A Little Bit About the Wines 323

Acknowledgments

WRITING A BOOK ON THE vast subject of the biblical culinary world while keeping it experiential and enjoyable has been mostly exhilarating, but occasionally intimidating. What began as a snapshot of the food and wine in the time of Jesus became a long-lens, panoramic view spanning centuries that exposed the rites, rituals, and traditions handed down through generations and cultures.

I am grateful for the writers and researchers who unearthed this ancient world and brought it to life so that we could get a glimpse of the history of food with its beginnings in the Garden, from gatherers to growers, and from sustenance to celebration. They uncovered the story of wine for us, which is equally as fascinating, shedding light on the millennia of grape growers from the first vineyard planted to all the wine-making pioneers whose wisdom and skills have left an indelible mark on society.

What Would Jesus Pair? would not have come to life without the enthusiasm and encouragement of my publisher, Tom Freiling. The moment I pitched my idea to you, you wholeheartedly embraced it and once again shared your unique vision for this book, paving the way to bring it to fruition. Your insight is invaluable. I truly appreciate the talented team of Freiling Publishing—thank you.

My husband, Rob, my most ardent supporter in this crazy, wonderful life, you deserve credit for consistently motivating me to reach my full potential and then some. I know it's often difficult living with a wine snob, but I hold you responsible for creating this monster. Spencer and Alec, my dear sons—my Renaissance men and biggest fans—your love for me and for family is a driving force. I admire your curiosity and desire to live life to the fullest. I am amazed by how you brightly shine the light of Christ for others to see.

I grew up in a family that appreciates tradition and shares enthusiasm for quality food and the celebration of wine—this too has been a source of motivation. Thank you for being part of my story, for sharing your recipes, culinary gifts, and an occasional bottle of wine—or two.

The Messiah family has been a blessing to me. The love and support I have received from so many of you has made a difference in my life. I appreciate your heartfelt prayers and kind words of encouragement. I especially want to thank Marcia Claesson for sharing your time and journalistic talent with me over the years. Pastors John, Dustin, and Andy, not only have you brought the love of Christ to life for your flock, but you have been enthusiastic advocates and truly good friends to my family and me.

Acknowledgments

There are countless more people to thank, but mostly I am in gratitude to my loving Father, Triune God, who has revealed to me a deep love for His people through the good gifts of creation.

Introduction

*You cause the grass to grow for the livestock
and plants for man to cultivate,
that he may bring forth food from the earth
and wine to gladden the heart of man,
oil to make his face shine
and bread to strengthen man's heart.*
—Psalm 104:14-15

IN THE BEGINNING, IN A lush garden, God provided a bounty for His creation that was beyond imagination. And ever since, civilization has enjoyed all that has sprung from the earth for our benefit. While every gift of nature is a blessing on its own, we simply cannot help but transform food into something more than mere sustenance as we are imbued with the creative characteristics of God—we are made in His image. The very essence of bread and wine transcends nature and enters our faith. Through bread and wine, we see that God is at work in all things.

A meal is elevated by a lofty loaf of crusty bread and a bottle of handcrafted wine. It nourishes both body and soul. We are inherently united when we gather around the table with family, friends, and even strangers.

What Would Jesus Pair?

I received my very first cookbook from my mother's best friend as a high school graduation gift; it was *The Joy of Cooking*. Today, forty-some years later, stained, earmarked, and now falling apart, it bears the marks of my love affair with cooking. Planning a special meal or event is something I do with great pleasure. Searching out the perfect dish for an occasion to be perfectly paired with wine brings joy to my soul. Chopping and sautéing, while swirling, sniffing, and sipping a delicious glass of vin du jour is a religious experience in itself which invariably brings me a little closer to heaven.

When I think of bread and wine, I think of Jesus. We are connected to one another through the culinary experience—we are connected to Jesus through bread and wine at His table. As I examined the significance of the Lord's Supper, I became acutely aware of the thousands of years of history, tradition, and ritual in its wake. I discovered the Lord's Supper in light of the Passover—a joy-filled celebration commemorating the Exodus and God's saving grace.

I wanted to know more about Jesus, the Son of God, who came down from heaven in the form of a man. Jesus traveled, He slept, He laughed and cried, and He prepared and shared meals. As a winemaker, I've often wondered what the wine He drank tasted like, and how it was made. On Sundays at church, sitting in the front row, my husband and I can smell the communion wine when the lid is taken off the trays of mini glasses. Surely the first century wine

Introduction

Jesus presented to His disciples in the upper room didn't smell or taste anything like the twenty-first century wine we have come to appreciate.

I originally set out to write a first-century travelog following the Eastern Mediterranean food and wine trail that Jesus and the disciples would have experienced together. I intended to provide a simple snapshot of the culinary culture of the times, but the events of those few short years in Jesus' life revealed much more. The culmination of events and the relationship between God, His chosen people, and the gifts of creation He so lavishly bestowed on humanity snapped into focus. You simply cannot isolate the religious, ethnic, or even culinary culture of the first century without understanding the origins and rich heritage that led up to this transformative time. Jesus is rooted in a family line that was blessed through bread, wine, and even vineyards as far back as 1,800 years prior to Abraham, the father of the nation.

The origins of ancient wine were established at the beginning of time and embrace the story of Jesus every step of the way. Jesus Himself declared; *I am the Bread of Life*, and *I am the Vine*. He used imagery that the people would be familiar with, and it told of a deeper relationship with them as it pointed to His covenant promise.

What did Jesus eat and drink? The Eastern Mediterranean is a rich land of culinary delights even today. The Holy Land can still be considered as a land flowing with milk and honey, of dates and figs, of pomegranates, olives, and... grapes. This place is the cradle of wine civilization. Some rabbinical scholars have suggested that perhaps Eve was not tempted by an apple, but a grape.

And what of the first disciples called by Jesus? They were fishermen. Fish are a gift from the sea. Jesus cooked fish, multiplied fish, and filled the nets of those first followers when they had come up empty. Fish are central to the Mediterranean diet and remain as a classic symbol of all Christians today that was established in the first century.

Food has played a major role in the rites and rituals of our ancestors. It was offered up at the temple, it was sacred, it was life. The Passover Seder has always been celebrated around a meal, a meal that is a transformational blessing nourishing our very souls. Food and wine tastes good for a reason, it tastes good because we are meant to enjoy it. It is a good gift from God—and a love language in itself.

Cultures are defined by their customs and the food they prepare and eat. I grew up in a family surrounded by culinary traditions and the wine elevated our meal to a celebratory event. I pray you rekindle a passion for your family traditions as you journey with my family and me, and the many generations of the Bible to the very beginning where God provided all that His creation required— in the Garden.

Introduction

What did the first bread and wine taste like? How was it made? I invite you to explore the culinary culture—the food and the wine—of the Bible and to break bread around the table that unites all people. I invite you to the meal of a lifetime—with Jesus.

Cheers!

Prologue

A RHYTHM OF WAVES LAPPING against the weathered slats of their fishing boat lulled the brothers into a familiar daze. It had been a long night out on the sea; they were hungry and tired. The sun was peering over the horizon as they returned with nets brimming. They were happy with their haul.

What they thought would be another ordinary day, turned out to be the most extraordinary day of their lives. Everything was about to change in ways beyond imagination. Heading back to shore, they could see a man walking by the sea. From that moment on, the world would never be the same again.

> *While walking by the Sea of Galilee, he saw two brothers, Simon (who is called Peter) and Andrew his brother, casting a net into the sea, for they were fishermen. And he said to them, "Follow me, and I will make you fishers of men." Immediately they left their nets and followed him.* —Matthew 4:18-20

Two ordinary fishermen, Peter and Andrew, were the first among whom Jesus called to follow Him. The livelihood of these initial disciples would be changed dramatically; they had been fishing for what we know today as tilapia on the Sea of Galilee, but from then on, they would be fishers of men out in the world. Immediately afterward, others were called and dropped everything without hesitation to follow Jesus far and wide.

The Bible doesn't tell us this, but it's likely that Peter and Andrew made their decision to follow Jesus over a breakfast of fish and wine. How do I know this? Fish were plentiful and wine was the most abundant beverage mentioned in Scripture. Nearly everyone in the Bible drank wine—including Jesus.

What kind of wine did Jesus and the disciples drink? What kind of food did they eat? It is through thousands of years of history and heritage that we get a taste of the times. The wine and food they experienced is at the heart of this journey and I bring it to you with modern, twenty-first century recipes based on the ancient traditions and an understanding of the wine to pair with the food.

Have you ever had a glass of wine with a dish that brought out the best of both? There is nothing quite as delightful as when food and wine is perfectly paired together. It makes me wonder, "What would Jesus pair?"

Section I

Explore the identity of Jesus as He walked the earth over two thousand years ago and as it relates to the traditions of celebrating the gift of wine and bread with a deeper biblical and spiritual understanding.

1

THE REAL JESUS

And he was seeking to see who Jesus was, but on account of the crowd he could not... —Luke 19:3

IF YOU WERE STANDING NEXT to Jesus, would you recognize Him; could you pick Him out of a crowd? Have you ever wondered what He looked like? What He sounded like, what He said? Who was Jesus really? In the Scripture verse above, it was Zacchaeus, the chief tax collector of the city of Jericho, who climbed a sycamore tree to get a glimpse of Jesus. He was curious. I would be curious too; I'd climb the tallest mountain just to see Jesus—that would surely be a mountaintop experience. The Gospel of Luke says that Jesus rescued Zacchaeus from his greed and subsequently he became an ardent and generous follower. Jesus had charisma.

I studied art history in college and continue to enjoy an appreciation of fine art—especially the more classical styles. I have seen countless paintings of Christ in museums, churches, and cathedrals both abroad and here in the United States; I have to say one of my favorite representations is an inlaid, wooden relief of Jesus from India that my husband and I bid on and won at an auction. We keep this unique piece of art on an easel in prominent view. I love this depiction of Jesus because it looks as if He's looking at me with a loving, gentle smile surrounded by His sheep—the kind Shepherd tending His flock. Is this what Jesus really looked like? I hope so.

There's some indication of what Christ looked like in the single most studied artifact—the Shroud of Turin. It is a centuries-old, linen cloth that bears the image of a man. It's the same man we believe to be Jesus of Nazareth. This precious shroud is the cloth that likely wrapped His crucified body when placed in the tomb; the image of His face and part of His body was left behind by what is thought to be the result of a burst of light—a vacuum of UV radiation—at the moment He was resurrected. It truly provides a good likeness of what the Lord really looked like. Although proof of what He looked like is not essential to have a relationship with Him, once you start putting a facial likeness to Jesus, it piques curiosity, we desire to know more about Him on a personal level, to know what His life was actually like.

> *Have this mind among yourselves, which is yours in Christ Jesus, who, though he was in the form of God, did not count equality with God a thing to be grasped, but*

emptied himself, by taking the form of a servant, being born in the likeness of men. —Philippians 2:5-7

I am fascinated to know more about Jesus, the Son of God, who came down from heaven in the form of a man and gave His life for humanity. What did He actually say and do? Did He laugh and cry? What did He eat and drink at home in Galilee or when He traveled? Jesus was anything but ordinary, but He lived in an ordinary way as a man here on earth. There are many years—the years between His childhood and His ministry—that are lost to records, and we don't know much about this most prominent figure in history other than He was a carpenter.

In the beginning was the Word, and the Word was with God, and the Word was God. He was in the beginning with God. —John 1:1-2

There is much we do know because of Scripture. The red-letter words (those printed in red in some publications of the Bible) are His very words recorded in the New Testament. In His own words, Jesus gives us insight into many truths through His sermons, conversations with His disciples and others, and even how He teaches them how to pray. *"Pray then like this: 'Our Father in heaven, hallowed be your name. Your kingdom come, your will be done, on earth as it is in heaven. Give us this day our daily bread, ...'"*

(Mark 6:9-13). The substance of this prayer withstands time, and the metaphor of bread points us to a much larger theme throughout the Bible.

Through His own words and those of the apostles we gain knowledge of what Jesus did especially in the Synoptic Gospels of Matthew, Mark, and Luke, and also the Gospel of John which explicitly reveals Who Jesus was. John was the utmost authority of the four, as he was *the one whom Jesus loved the most* (John 13:23). We even get a glimpse of many aspects of His daily life including some of what He ate and drank. And yes, to answer the previous question, *"Did Jesus cry?"* John tells us, *"He wept"* (John 11:35). Jesus had emotions—He was fully God and fully man.

Jesus, when he began his ministry, was about thirty years of age, being the son (as was supposed) of Joseph…
—Luke 3:23

The first account of Jesus as an adult is when He began His ministry after being baptized in the Jordan river by His cousin, John the Baptist. John didn't drink wine (or any alcohol) and lived on wild honey and locusts—not exactly a culinary delight, even for the times, but it was convenient and kosher. It is right after this event that Jesus called His first disciples, Simon (Peter) and Andrew, fishing on the sea of Galilee, and soon thereafter ten more were called to become "the twelve." From this point on

Jesus would spend most of His time with these students who would soon carry out the mission of building God's church on earth.

We tend to not think of Jesus as a mortal man, and rightfully so because He is God. But we must consider what Paul tells us in Philippians—*He was sent down from heaven and took the form of a man;* He was a man with a single-minded mission to save humanity. As a man, He had human physiology and as a result, there were certain necessities required to sustain His physical body; He had to sleep, eat, and drink, and as He was a first-century Jew, you have to wonder what that looked like.

Many people think of Jesus as always pensive and pious. Movies often portray Him as aloof and starry-eyed, looking off into the heavens and wearing gleaming white robes. It is common to envision Jesus only as a deity in the glow of His heavenly existence. And although He is a deity—the God of all creation who deserves all glory and honor—that's not how He was living as a man among men here on earth. While He did have a serious side, I imagine Him a loving man who exuded a certain joyfulness, He was personable and surely affable. He had good relationships with His disciples in those few short years they spent together, and in that time, they laughed, cried, and prayed. I love to imagine Jesus as Jonathan Roumie portrays Him in the Dallas Jenkins series, *The Chosen*.

What Would Jesus Pair?

Many things occurred in those three years Jesus spent with the disciples before He was crucified. As they traveled together and set up camp, healed the sick, and performed miracles, they were living life together—real life that was gritty and often difficult. What did He and his disciples talk about? There was a lot of teaching going on in the daily affairs, but I have to believe that there was laughter and joy mixed with the seriousness, and sometimes even sadness. Many of the conversations Jesus had transpired around meals, around food and wine. The real Jesus drank real wine. I can picture Him at a dinner table with His close friends Mary, Martha, and Lazarus truly enjoying their friendship—even when Martha was busy and distracted (Luke 10:40). The meal was to be celebrated as a gift, one that more than just sustained the body.

Most of the time Jesus ate ordinary meals with common people, just as you and I enjoy everyday meals with our families at home. But there were extraordinary occasions that called for community like feasts and banquets as we see throughout the Bible. Most traditions carried over from the Jewish culture in their rites and rituals, and for Jesus, it was right up through His last meal—The Last Supper which was the Passover Seder. Otherwise, Jesus and His followers ate what was available depending on where they were at the time. They traveled through various geographical regions which offered different kinds of food and wine and it was often prepared for them by their host. Experiencing such culinary diversity must have provided great pleasure, it was a change from the cuisine they were accustomed to in Galilee where they spent much of their time.

> *And a scribe came up and said to him, "Teacher, I will follow you wherever you go." And Jesus said to him, "Foxes have holes, and birds of the air have nests, but the Son of Man has nowhere to lay his head."*
> —Matthew 8:19-20

Jesus claimed to have no home—at least not here on earth. He counted on the hospitality of others for meals especially when He was on the road. He was invited to dinners and even banquets with all kinds of people from lowly farmers and fishermen to wealthy Pharisees. I often think about what I would serve the Son of God if He were to come over for dinner; there's no question that the wine selection would be second to none. I could tell you this for sure, if I hosted Jesus in my home, Gordon Ramsey would have nothing on me.

Wouldn't it be fun to share a meal with Jesus and the disciples, and hear their reactions to the unique flavors in the herbs and spices of a certain region, or their preference for a particular wine? What were their favorite meals? How often were they treated to a dessert like sweet fig cake?

What Would Jesus Pair?

I like to envision Jesus—the Son of God, the Master Creator—as a culinary aficionado, enjoying all the gifts of creation: fruits and nuts, fish and fowl, cheese... and wine. Frankly, it begs the question, "What would Jesus pair?"

2

The Gift of Wine

If food is the body of good living, wine is its soul.
—Clifton Fadiman

When my husband and I are fortunate to be invited to someone's home for dinner or a party, we always bring a favorite bottle of wine to bless the host. It doesn't matter to us if they choose to pop the cork at the time or if they save it for another special occasion. Regardless, one thing that the gift does, in nearly every circumstance, is to open up lively conversation about wine, creating an atmosphere of joy—because who doesn't love wine.

Swirl, sniff, sip, savor... It's heaven in a glass. Wine is an undeniable gift from God—the result of His magnificent creation and a tangible reminder of His love for us. From the moment the grafted grapevine is planted in prepared soil, you can see God's hand at work. The life of a vine and its resulting fruitfulness is truly something to behold. Having lived on a vineyard for ten years, I can attest to the beauty of the vineyard in the awe-inspiring formation of grape clusters from bud to berry, and the thrill of harvest. Harvest is just the beginning of the transformational process a grape will endure, becoming a stunning glass of wine.

> *Taste and see that the Lord is good.* —Psalm 34:8

Most people would be surprised by how much attention is given to wine in the Bible; wine is mentioned about 235 times, more than any other beverage. It's fascinating to see how wine plays a central role in our relationship with God. How can that be so? Along with viticulture, it's a very significant theme throughout all of Scripture from Genesis to Revelation. We see that wine and vineyards are part of God's rich blessings bestowed upon His people right from the beginning in Genesis where wine is considered a good gift of creation. In Genesis 2, God plants and then places His creation in a lush garden and invites them to eat and enjoy its fruit.

Wine in Scripture

Is wine really a blessed gift in Scripture? Most certainly it is. In the Bible, there are forty-seven references of wine in abundance as examples of God's blessings, and the lack of it as a curse. Psalm 104:15 says very clearly that God gave wine to *"gladden the heart of man."* Wine has had multiple uses in the ancient faith community, and still plays an important role in the life of the church today; it has been used as food, for medicinal purposes, and in religious rites, rituals, and celebrations. The Jewish people drank it at Passover, and from early on it was used in their offerings and sacrifices (Genesis 35:14, Numbers 28:7). Jesus, observing the Passover the night before He was crucified, presented a cup of wine and invited the disciples to, *"Drink in remembrance of me"* (1 Corinthians 11:25).

> *"I tell you I will not drink again of this fruit of the vine until that day when I drink it new with you in my Father's kingdom."* —Matthew 26:29

The New Testament curtain draws to a close in Revelation, the final book of the Bible, as it is revealed that those who *know* Christ will be feasting with Him at the wedding supper of the Lamb in heaven (*"my Father's Kingdom"*). We have had a foretaste of the feast to come. Jesus drank His last wine on earth and presented it as a gift. The gift of wine (His blood) along with bread (His body) is the elemental blessing from God in the new covenant promise. Wine is one of the gifts of nature that was used in offerings and sacrifice from early on and throughout time. It is through bread and wine that we share communion with God and an opportunity to commune spiritually with one another.

What Would Jesus Pair?

On the third day there was a wedding at Cana in Galilee, and the mother of Jesus was there. Jesus also was invited to the wedding with his disciples. —John 2:1-2

Weddings were the best of celebrations and the wine served is a long-standing symbol of joy. Jesus, along with His mother and His disciples, were invited guests to a wedding feast at Cana in Galilee. A terrible thing happened, the host ran out of wine. This was a major faux pas and would cause not only great embarrassment, but especially shame and dishonor to the family. Jesus, the source of abundance, performed His first public miracle and provided the best wedding gift—He turned the stone jars of water into well over a hundred gallons of wine, and not just any wine. Jesus appeared as the true bridegroom at the wedding feast who served the best wine, a gift of God's abounding goodness and grace.

When the master of the feast tasted the water now become wine, and did not know where it came from (though the servants who had drawn the water knew), the master of the feast called the bridegroom and said to him, "Everyone serves the good wine first, and when people have drunk freely, then the poor wine. But you have kept the good wine until now." —John 2:9-10

The Gift of Wine

Blessed Generations

> *And Melchizedek, king of Salem brought out bread and wine. (He was a priest of God Most High.) And he blessed him and said, "Blessed be Abram by God Most High, Possessor of heaven and earth; and blessed be God Most High, who has delivered your enemies into your hand!"*
> —Genesis 14:18-20

We see wine as a blessing profoundly played out in the four-generation story of Abraham, his only son Isaac, his grandson Jacob, and great-grandsons Joseph and Judah. The blessed provision began when Melchizedek, a great and righteous ruler, greeted Abraham with bread and wine and thereby blessed him. The blessings continue in this family line down to Joseph and Judah, and we see the promise of Israel and its favor become apparent through him specifically. Joseph became an ambassador of wine— he was looked upon as the advisor to the chief wine expert in Israel, and ultimately inherited a land of *"great harvests and plenty of wine."* Joseph eventually became a prominent wine merchant.

Fast forward about 600 years and we come to the story of the wilderness wanderings. After forty years of wandering the dusty, barren desert, the Israelites arrived at the border of a new land. Moses sent out scouts to explore the land and they came upon Eschol which means *"the valley of grape clusters."* This they knew to be the long-awaited land overflowing with milk and honey—The Promised Land. They cut and carried a single grape cluster back to their people along with figs and pomegranates. Moses would bring them to the land filled with vineyards and olive trees. *"That place was called the Valley of Eshcol because of the cluster that the people of Israel cut down from there."* (Numbers 13:23-24)

The fifth book of the Bible, Deuteronomy, mentions the term "bless" forty-six times (in Hebrew). God promised many blessings to Israel in this book if only they would obey His commands. Many of those blessings included the "blessed" fruit of the ground, successful farming, bountiful harvests, and prosperity. So, it shouldn't be surprising that at the end of this book in Chapter 33, Moses, just before his death, bestowed his final blessing over the whole tribe of Israel. This blessing included living in a land of plentiful grain, wine, and olive oil *"whose heavens drop down dew."* (Deuteronomy 33:28-29).

We also see time and time again in Scripture that a lack of wine is a curse from the Lord for those who did not obey. Deuteronomy 28 especially spells out the blessings and the curses that followers of God can expect upon a nation that turns away from God's law. Those who do not obey, are plagued: *"You will plant vineyards and cultivate them but you will not drink the wine or gather the grapes, because worms will eat them* (Deuteronomy 28:39)." A lack of wine, it would seem, was their punishment.

> *Neither is new wine put into old wineskins. If it is, the skins burst and the wine is spilled and the skins are destroyed. But new wine is put into fresh wineskins, and so both are preserved."* —Matthew 9:17

I love the metaphor of wineskins that Jesus illustrates for us in this verse. Wineskins were made of animal skins simply to hold wine. Jesus is saying that His arrival as the Messiah has begun the new era of the kingdom of heaven. He is the "new wine." The old ways of Judaism are like the old wineskins—they dry out and burst when new wine ferments in them, and the wine is forfeited. He clarifies that the ways of the kingdom through Him will no longer be in accord with the old religious practices and observances. The new wine represents the innermost characteristics of a new Christian heart; the new wineskin is essentially our new bodily temple housing the Holy Spirit as Jesus destroyed the physical temple and rebuilt it in three days (Matthew 26:61).

Why does Jesus use wineskins as a metaphor in Matthew 19:7? Wine played such an important part in the culture and symbolism of the church that it was very recognizable. Jesus describes Himself as The One True Vine, *"I am the Vine, you are the branches"* (John 15:5). He is

The Vine Who produces fruit for all. Immediately after it's harvested, the fruit is crushed and the winemaking begins; metaphorically speaking, Jesus was crushed for us under death on the cross which opened the path of a new life for us—a new life in Christ—the new wine. Jesus prophetically points to the wine He offered at the Last Supper as His blood that would be poured out for us—His ultimate gift to save His people.

In the New Testament, wine is revealed as a symbol of Messianic blessing (relating to Jesus the Messiah) and which comes only through Him. The prophet Isaiah foretold that "On this *mountain the Lord of hosts will make for all peoples a feast of rich food, a feast of well-aged wine, of rich food full of marrow, of aged wine well refined.*" (Isaiah 25:6) This is yet another undeniable reference to a gift of blessed prosperity.

> *Honor the Lord with your wealth and with the firstfruits of all your produce; then your barns will be filled with plenty, and your vats will be bursting with wine.*
> —Proverbs 3:9-10

Plentiful wine is a gift from the Lord. Proverbs 3:9-10 reminds us that generosity toward God will be returned with *plenty* of food and wine (that which sustains us). Although our generosity should not be predicated on what we receive in return, those who honor God from their wealth can expect blessings (and in the case of this verse) *"vats bursting with wine."* Wine represents many things, but especially joy, celebration, and festivity, expressing the profusion of God's love for us—now that is a lavish gift. How do we as the benefactors of His abundance show our gratitude for such riches? We celebrate with joy, one of the nine "fruits" of the Spirit (Galatians 5:22-23)—partaking in all the good gifts from God our Father.

> *But the fruit of the Spirit is love, joy, peace, patience, kindness, goodness, faithfulness, gentleness, self-control; against such things there is no law.*
> —Galatians 5:22-23

Is it a coincidence that God created grapes with the natural ability to ferment into wine using yeast and all that He provided in nature? One could say that wine makes itself; it's imbued with this transformational attribute in its very DNA. Through the gift of wine, our cup of blessings overflows.

> *You cause the grass to grow for the livestock and plants for man to cultivate, that he may bring forth food from the earth and wine to gladden the heart of man, oil to make his face shine and bread to strengthen man's heart.*
> —Psalm 104:15

3

BREAD OF HEAVEN

Then the Lord said to Moses, "Behold, I am about to rain bread from heaven for you, and the people shall go out and gather a day's portion every day..."
—Exodus 1:4

WHO DOESN'T LOVE BREAD? My hubby and I honeymooned in London and Paris, and while we love so many things about London, we fell in love with the French cuisine. The very first priority, after dropping our luggage at the quaint Hotel Maison Colbert, was to seek out a classic, Parisian café for a carafe of wine with an accompaniment of cheese and a crusty baguette. I thought we arrived in heaven.

Modern day boulangeries (French bakeries), are the envy of the world and testament to the historical significance of bread in France. It even cost Marie Antoinette her head as a result of her insensitive utterance, *"Qu'ils mangent de la brioche"* meaning *"Let them eat cake!* (Or rather brioche, a rich bread made with eggs and butter) when she was told her starving peasant subjects didn't even have bread to eat. Like cooking and winemaking, the French wrote *the* book for making bread, and have perfected and preserved this artisanal craft since the Middle Ages. As Italy is respected as the cultural home of pizza, France is likewise renowned for quality bread.

This one food item is central to most diets across the world and eaten daily among all social classes. Bread is a universal staple in its various shapes and forms. Bread is many things beside nourishment, it's comfort and invokes nostalgia—the specific kind of bread you grew up with speaks to where you are from.

Pizza is a dish that has become popular around the world, with each culture giving it their unique twist. I grew up in New Jersey, the home of Frank Sinatra (the Patron Saint of the state), and pizza—real, authentic pizza. Don't bother to try to argue the subject with anyone from Jersey, you can't win. This is a serious subject. My family held a competition on who could make the best pizza dough; it was too dangerous to declare a winner.

Bread is an important food item in nearly every culture. I love to cook and one thing that stands out when exploring the cuisine of other countries and their culinary traditions is the emphasis on their respective styles of bread. Ciabatta invokes visions of Italian sandwiches, the thought of naan induces the headiness of aromatic Indian spices, marbled rye makes my mouth water for the rich food of a Jewish deli, and flatbread with hummus, olive tapenade, and cucumber yogurt dip is tantalizing.

What's an authentic Mexican meal without warm tortillas, southern fried chicken without cornbread, or Sunday brunch without bagels? And contrary to belief, bagels originated in Poland—not New York.

At Christmas each year, Rob and I host a *make your own gourmet grilled cheese and soup* party. A variety of artisan breads spill out of baskets to be individually paired with gourmet cheeses and meats and toasted on Panini grills. Homemade soup offerings include an onion gratinèe with Gruyère cheese and the pièce de ré·sis·tance—a crouton made from a crusty baguette. We love to watch everyone hanging around dipping their sandwiches in a cup of soup and sipping on their choice of wine.

I'm hard pressed to recall a meal served in a restaurant, at parties, or at home that did not include some style of bread; I even love food served in a bread bowl. Today, bread is offered in restaurants, grocery stores, and farmers' markets in many forms to meet different dietary needs, these include gluten free, yeast free, keto, vegan, cornbread, rice bread, bean bread, and ancient grain bread among others. Bread is truly the staff of life. There is bread for every person regardless of circumstances.

Up until recently, my youngest (kind of picky) son, Alec, all but lived on bread—nothing made him happier. While he has expanded his food horizons, it is still his go-to comfort food.

Ancient Bread

> *For the Lord your God is bringing you into a good land, a land of brooks of water, of fountains and springs, flowing out in the valleys and hills, a land of wheat and barley, of vines and fig trees and pomegranates, a land of olive trees and honey, a land in which you will eat bread without scarcity, in which you will lack nothing, a land whose stones are iron, and out of whose hills you can dig copper. And you shall eat and be full, and you shall bless the Lord your God for the good land he has given you.*
> —Deuteronomy 8:7-10

The Middle East is the cradle of agricultural endeavors, this is where bread became a staple as man progressed from gatherers to growers. Bread was at the heart of the Mediterranean diet and eaten daily. Biblically and practically, it was the most important food essential for life—when other food items ran out (like in the wilderness wanderings of the Exodus), bread sustained their lives. And when the bread was gone so was life.

God told His people that they *"will eat bread without scarcity"* in the Promised Land.

In the first century, bread was made every day except on the Sabbath for Jews—the day of rest. Most homes had ovens, and in the cities, there would have been community ovens shared by the citizens. The kind of bread one ate spoke of their respective social class. Barley bread was made by the poorest, and those with more resources made bread from wheat. The wealthiest ate white bread made from refined flour. It's interesting how the tides have turned; refined, white bread is now the cheapest of breads on the market—certainly not on the grocery lists of the wealthy. Artisan breads, unrefined, and with whole grains, are eaten by those who can afford it.

While there were different kinds of bread in the first century, most of it was large and flat. The Jews were likely introduced to leavened bread in Egypt, but unleavened bread remained an important part of their religious observances, feasts, and even sacrifices. For most of human history, bread has been synonymous with life—and not just to sustain physical life, but spiritual life.

> *Bread is a whole lot more than a mere food. A goodly loaf is the staff of life.* —Anon

Bread enjoys a long history with undeniable symbolic and religious connotations. For one thing, bread was considered a miracle. Two main ingredients made up common bread, water and flour. Have you ever made your own bread? Consider that the bread you have always made was consistently flat, but one day, you left your dough on the counter overnight and the next morning it was bigger.

What Would Jesus Pair?

If this surprised you and had never seen it happen before, you'd think it was magic… or a miracle.

What made it a seeming miracle was the yeast that existed naturally in the arid Mediterranean environment. Much like the fermentation of wine (the yeast feeds on the fruit sugar), yeast had a transformational effect on bread causing it to bubble and rise. Author, Maguelonne Toussaint-Samet, in her book, *A History of Food*, refers to bread as one in the fundamental trinity (the holy trinity) of food along with wine and olives because of their impact on Western civilization.

Lechem is the Hebrew word for bread and mentioned in the Old Testament 296 times in thirty of the thirty-nine books. That's a lot of bread. It makes you wonder why it is such a prevalent food throughout Scripture just as wine is the most consumed beverage. It's no mystery that bread was the most common and necessary food and not surprising that it still is today. It symbolizes many things including joy, hospitality, blessings, miracles, and life among others. Bread sustains life. What does it mean to you?

Even in modern history, when we look at the great depression era in this country (not all that long ago), it was the *breadlines* where the poverty stricken queued up for food. In modern day slang, *bread* and *dough* have associations with money made famous in the gangster movies of the 1930s and '40s. Bread was used as a bartered item in ancient cultures.

While Cecil B. Demille did not highlight it in his epic movie, *The Ten Commandments*, bread takes center stage in the ancient story of the Israelites' exodus from Egypt.

> *And the whole congregation of the people of Israel grumbled against Moses and Aaron in the wilderness, and the people of Israel said to them, "Would that we had died by the hand of the Lord in the land of Egypt, when we sat by the meat pots and ate bread to the full, for you have brought us out into this wilderness to kill this whole assembly with hunger." Then the Lord said to Moses, "Behold, I am about to rain bread from heaven for you, and the people shall go out and gather a day's portion every day…* —Exodus 16:2-4

Bread was God's miraculous gift to the Israelites as chronicled in the book of Exodus. These people had been enslaved by the Egyptians for 430 years and were finally set free after God's intervention through Moses. As they were making their way through the desert they began to starve. Of course, they began grumbling to Moses and Aaron, but God, in His great mercy, rained down manna—bread from heaven—every day. The Lord continued to feed them for forty years with this *food of angels* and it became their reminder that they were dependent on God.

And when the dew had gone up, there was on the face of the wilderness a fine, flake-like thing, fine as frost on the ground. When the people of Israel saw it, they said to one another, "What is it?" For they did not know what it was. And Moses said to them, "It is the bread that the Lord has given you to eat. —Exodus 16:13-15

While manna is considered *bread from heaven,* it's truly something unique that doesn't really seem to resemble bread at all. Moses provided some interesting details of this *food of angels:*

- it had to be collected before it melted by the heat of the sun
- it was a fine, flake-like thing, fine as frost on the ground and similar to a coriander seed in size, but white in color
- the Israelites ground it and shaped it into cakes, which were then baked—they tasted like cakes baked with oil
- raw manna had the flavor of wafers made with honey
- left over manna bred worms and was foul smelling

"This is what the Lord has commanded: 'Tomorrow is a day of solemn rest, a holy Sabbath to the Lord; bake what *you will bake and boil what you will boil, and all that is left over lay aside to be kept till the morning.'" So they laid it aside till the morning, as Moses commanded them, and it did not stink, and there were no worms in it. Moses said, 'Eat it today, for today is a Sabbath to the Lord; today you will not find it in the field. Six days you shall gather it, but on the seventh day, which is a Sabbath, there will be none.'"* —Exodus 16:23-26

While one could argue that it was the "Wonder Bread" of the time, manna was no ordinary bread that merely satiated physical hunger, it was a supernatural food that provided the Israelites divine nourishment. We don't have any recipes for the bread that was baked from this heavenly food, because we don't have the same form of manna that God sent to the Israelites. However, I share some recipes that you can make based on the bread that they likely would have eaten in "The Recipes" chapter.

Once the Israelites arrived in the Promised Land, manna no longer rained down from heaven as they were entering into, "*...a land of wheat and barley, of vines and fig trees and pomegranates, a land of olive trees and honey, a land in which you will eat bread without scarcity, in which you will lack nothing...*" (Deuteronomy 8:8-9).

Manna, with its spiritual significance, makes its way into the New Testament as we start to understand what Jesus was saying when He spoke of *the manna of the exodus* and that He would give *new manna* to those who believe in Him.

A Symbol of Hospitality

When we entertain in our home, we welcome our guests with a glass of wine and appetizers. Our favorites are cheese fondue with a French baguette, a charcuterie of meats, cheeses, nuts, olives, and... breads; we often like to serve Italian bruschetta drenched in olive oil and topped with garlicky, chopped tomatoes. Can you think of anything bread doesn't go with? I think you'll enjoy some of the appetizer pairing ideas and recipes provided in Section VI.

Bread is no doubt a symbol of hospitality. It brings people together in fellowship and provides blessings as we see in the story of Abraham. In Genesis 18, Moses tells how Abraham (known as Abram at the time) shared *a morsel of bread,* along with curds and milk, and had a calf prepared for a meal for three visitors—one of which was the Lord. And we cannot forget that Abraham received the blessings of Melchizedek, King of Salem, when he, in a gesture of hospitality, brought out bread and wine from his tent to welcome, and specifically bless, Abraham.

Jewish meals still begin with the blessing over bread and then the breaking and sharing of the bread together. The blessing would have been widely known to Jesus and his followers in the first century: *"Blessed is the Holy One of*

Israel, Sovereign of all that is who brings forth the bread from the ground."

God is great. God is good. And we thank Him for our food. By His hands we all are fed, give us Lord our daily bread. Amen

This is the mealtime prayer of my childhood. Do you recognize it? Most Judeo-Christians would recognize the words, if not in its entirety, then at least the first sentence. While "our daily bread" is part of the prayer—The Lord's Prayer—that Jesus taught His disciples to pray, we can identify with it as something relevant to us today as our daily needs are met physically and spiritually.

The Greeks and Egyptians are paid homage by the culinary history of bread. In diving into the subject of ancient bread, I was overwhelmed (and always hungry) that the history of bread alone would fill the pages of an enormous volume.

In the history of art there are periods when bread seems so beautiful that it nearly gets into museums.

—Janet Flanner

It is a subject of poetry, literary works, philosophy, and mythology. Throughout time, songs have been written about bread—*Bread* was even the name of a rock band of the 1970s. Plato, Aristotle, and Hippocrates among other historical figures expounded on belief systems, values, symbols, and signs of this one, basic food item. It even has extensive meaning throughout history tied to fertility in many ancient and modern cultures. The Spanish word for yeast is *madre*, meaning mother; many other languages have words for yeast and bread with similar connotation.

I found that bread in Scripture is an inexhaustible subject. Back to the far reaches of creation, bread alone has dominated as a symbol of life. As we look forward through the books of the New Testament, bread remains, along with wine, as the very essence of life through Christ—*the New Manna, the Bread of Heaven.*

I cannot think of another food item that is more prevalent, versatile, and universal than bread; it's all that and comfort too. What is life without bread?"

4

BREAD OF LIFE

Because there is one bread, we who are many are one body, for we all partake of the one bread.
—1 Corinthians 10:17

THE CHURCH I GREW UP in was relatively small and old. As an adult in my late twenties, I became very active in my congregation; among other areas of involvement, my mother and I served on the altar care committee together. Setting out the wafers for communion one Sunday, I thought, "Wouldn't it be nice to have special, home-baked bread instead of these little, generic discs?"

Communion wafers are nothing to write home about. They are dry and tasteless, and often stick to the roof of your mouth. The thimble full of wine that follows is not enough to assuage this dilemma—and it's usually not very good either. These modern-day communion elements are nothing like the bread and wine of Jesus' time—my, how we have regressed since the first century.

I approached my pastor with the idea of providing special, home-made bread in place of wafers and he loved it. After he set me loose on this task, I researched and experimented with several recipes; I found just the right one—a braided butter bread. It was beautiful with three braided strands to represent the trinity, it was delicious, and best of all it didn't crumble when broken on the altar to give to those partaking in communion. It was such a hit that I taught a class on making this bread and shared the recipe and the responsibility. The aroma in my home was heavenly with yeast as the dough rose in a tea-towel-covered bowl on the radiator and then baked to perfection. I can still smell it.

> *I've heard it said that when you die you enter a room of bright light, and that you can smell bread baking just around the corner.* —Rick Bass

Sitting in the pews of that same church as a child, I was fascinated by the simple Moravian glass windows etched with the "I Am" sayings of Jesus that surrounded me. In my book, *Jesus in the Vineyard*, I describe how the specific window that read, "I Am the Vine," captivated me and held my attention because of its beauty and mystery. I knew there was hidden meaning which I didn't understand at such a young age, but I trusted God would reveal it to me someday—and He did in the most profound and personal way.

Likewise, there was another window that caught my attention, "I Am the Bread of Life."

Bread encompassed many things practically, spiritually, and prophetically in the Old Testament, and it was present since the beginning. Biblically, bread has a variety of meanings and rich symbolism including provision and survival, life, salvation, and forgiveness. It is central to our lives and so important that we still celebrate it today in both our Jewish and Christian faiths—especially in the Passover Seder and respectively the Lord's Supper. Bread is transformational.

Bread, in its many forms and religious symbolism, made a natural transition into the books of the New Testament. The word bread (and its various iterations) is mentioned nearly 100 times in the twenty-seven books of the New Testament and continues through the close of Scripture in Revelation (2:17), *"To the one who conquers I will give some of the hidden manna…"*

I Am the Bread of Life

> *Jesus said to them, "I am the bread of life; whoever comes to me shall not hunger, and whoever believes in me shall never thirst. But I said to you that you have seen me and yet do not believe.* —John 6:35-36

These are the very words Jesus spoke to the crowds that followed Him to the other side of the Sea of Galilee—and I believe He was also saying it for the benefit of disciples so that they too believe, truly believe. Remember Thomas? He had doubts even when the risen Jesus was standing right in front of him.

It was the Apostle John who gave this *heavenly food* the most attention in all of the New Testament. The miracles illustrate what Jesus did, but what of His true identity? Although we see Christ's omniscient power through His miracles, John gets to the heart of His identity in the *signs* provided by the specific miracles chronicled in his Gospel (*so that you may believe*) and specifically in His "I Am" statements.

In John's Gospel, the Greek words *ego eimi* (I Am) are uttered by Jesus twenty-six times. These two words, "I Am," have far reaching meaning and impact and they all point to His redemptive mission. Jesus made seven "I Am" declarations.

- I Am the Bread of Life
- I Am the Light of the World
- I Am the Gate
- I Am the Good Shepherd
- I Am the Resurrection and the Life
- I Am the Way and the Truth and the Life
- I Am the Vine

Feeding the 5,000

There have been many occasions when we've had unexpected guests pop over for a visit. Providing wine was never an issue with a cellar full of vintages and varietals for every palate, and I learned how to be creative and improvise with wine-friendly snacks. Nothing goes better with wine than cheese, so we always have a variety—just in case. I've put on a quick spread in a pinch so many times that I can do it without worry. But I never had to pull off a miracle like Jesus did feeding 5,000 people with only five loaves of bread and two fish.

Crowds had grown to hear Jesus after He healed the sick, and the Passover was at hand. *"Jesus said to Philip, 'Where are we to buy bread, so that these people may eat?' He said this to test him, for he himself knew what he would do."* (John 6:5-6). After a young boy offered up his picnic lunch, Jesus miraculously turned his five barley loaves and two fish into enough food to feed 5,000 people—and had leftovers. What Jesus provides is not only enough, but also more than enough.

The miracle of feeding over 5,000 people with such little provision was immediately followed by His walking on water (John 6:16-21). The disciples got into a boat to cross the sea and a storm arose; they were more than concerned. When they saw Jesus walking toward them on the water, they became frightened. Jesus quelled their fears, but not before they heard His voice, *"It is I; do not be afraid."*

"I Am" is the personal, sacred name of God.

It was the very next day after performing two miracles that Jesus declared, *"I Am the Bread of Life."* The disciples would have recognized His meaning and would have made the correlation—Jesus, as the Messiah, was providing life-giving bread, just as God, His Father, had provided life-giving manna to the Israelites.

> *Jesus then said to them, "Truly, truly, I say to you, it was not Moses who gave you the bread from heaven, but my Father gives you the true bread from heaven. For the bread of God is he who comes down from heaven and gives life to the world." They said to him, "Sir, give us this bread always."* —John 6:32-34

"I am the Bread of Life" is the very first of the seven "I Am" statements Jesus made. In all of the ways bread has been used in Scripture, this instance is the most important. This simple metaphor, *"I am the Bread of Life"* is part of a bigger picture with far reaching biblical, historical, and life-giving relevance. Jesus made this declaration to the very crowds that continued to follow Him, those whom He had just fed the day before. But what kind of bread did they really want?

Jesus, in feeding the multitudes, was essentially providing a Passover meal (as the Passover was at hand), and it points to a bigger feast, a feast in which we are all invited to His table where He offers Himself for us, *"...this is my body given for you."*

Here He feeds His people with the *Bread of Life*. Those who receive this bread receive more than just sustenance, they receive an everlasting food that cannot perish from the Son of God. Bread is unmistakably transformational. The Bread of Heaven becomes the Bread of Life.

If we are to grasp the enormity of Jesus' identity in His declaration, *"I am the Bread of Life,"* then we must look back to the Israelites wilderness wanderings from the book of Exodus: *Then the Lord said to Moses, "Behold, I am about to rain bread from heaven for you, and the people shall go out and gather a day's portion every day"* (Exodus 16:4). Jesus studied and intimately knew the Scriptures; the story of the Exodus would have been most prominent in the life of the Jews.

The story of the Exodus is one of promise and rescue from slavery to a new life through sacrifices; God keeps His promises with a *new covenant* by way of a *new exodus*—through the sacrifice of His Son, Jesus. He redeemed us from death and gave us new life through the Bread of Life.

Jesus himself is the new spiritual food. The sacred elements of the Lord's Supper are His body and blood made present in bread and wine.

Breaking Bread

When we break bread and give it to each other, fear vanishes and God becomes very close. —Henri Nouwen

Many years ago, my father, who loved to bake bread, was invited by my sister's father-in-law, Ugo, to bake Easter bread with him. Ugo had a second kitchen in his basement. When my father arrived, everything was laid out and ready to begin—including fifty-pound bags of flour. They were not going to make just a few loaves, they were going to make enough to feed a small army! Perhaps they thought they were going to feed the 5,000. It took days to make an abundance of yeast bread that would be shared with friends and family; my father was truly in heaven.

When we lived in California, Ugo's grand-daughter Sophia, my niece, would drive up the coast from Los Angeles for the weekend armed with her grandpa's hand-cranked pasta maker. She taught my boys the art of pasta and to this day they crank out some of the best pasta I've ever had. We loved gathering around the kitchen, making pasta dough, and listening to our favorite music with a glass of wine in hand. Dinner was a veritable feast; what's pasta without the bread to sop up all the goodness, and a perfectly paired bottle of Chianti Classico. We have fond memories of breaking bread together as we gathered with happy hearts.

> *"And day by day, attending the temple together and breaking bread in their homes, they received their food with glad and generous hearts."* —Acts 2:46

> *This gesture, breaking bread together, has a rich meaning. It's a symbol of familiarity, of welcome, of openness, as well as a gesture signifying peace and friendship. We think of it as having a meal together, which it is, but the language of breaking bread together seems to have much more significance, because the emphasis is more on the connection between the people than on the fact that they are eating. It is more about the relationship than the food.* —Fr. Peter Wigton[1]

Bread is a food for every person regardless of class or culture—it's the one thing that crosses all borders and barriers, and I would dare to say it even unites us.

Jesus and His disciples shared a lot of meals, and His very last meal on earth was with His *twelve* and centered around bread and wine. He shared the Passover with them and gave it a new meaning—He became the food that builds unity, He was building deeper relationships.

---

[1] *News-Review*, "Lift up your Hearts: Breaking Bread Together,", 2020, petoskeynews.com.

Luke 22:15 tells us, *"And he said to them, 'I have earnestly desired to eat this Passover with you before I suffer.'"*

Suffer and die He did. But the Messiah was a king that was to take the throne, not die like a criminal. And that is what perplexed the two disciples on the road to Emmaus returning home after the Passover (Luke 24:13-32).

Even after Jesus approached the disciples and walked and talked with them, they still didn't recognize Him. Could you imagine walking and talking with Jesus and not recognizing Him? How did these two disciples not know they were with Jesus?

It wasn't until later that day when they shared a meal with Jesus that reality set in, *"when he was at table with them, he took the bread and blessed, and broke it, and gave it to them,"* and finally, *"their eyes were opened and they recognized him; and he vanished out of their sight* (Luke 24:30-31).

> *Then they told what had happened on the road, and how he was known to them in the breaking of the bread.*
> —Luke 24:35

Jesus didn't want to reveal his identity until they *broke bread* together. He wants us to recognize Him in this seemingly simple act—He wants us to recognize Him as we gather in the breaking of bread. We become one in the body of Christ when we break bread together. Bread truly does unite us with one another and with God.

The custom of breaking bread was not new to Jesus as He grew up celebrating the Passover with unleavened bread, an essential element commanded by God and to be celebrated. To "break bread" means to share a meal with others, breaking off pieces of your loaf to make certain there is enough for all. When Jesus ate with His disciples, He gave them pieces of bread; the bread, however, was hard so it had to be broken rather than torn unlike softer, modern bread that we are accustomed to today.

Sharing meals and unity have always been a very important part of Jewish family and community life over the ages, and it still is today. This, however, is not only reserved for the Jewish culture, a quick glance at the culinary customs of all cultures reveals a universal, human need to *break bread* together. Bread feeds the soul.

Give Us This Day Our Daily Bread

"To those of us who believe that all of life is sacred every crumb of bread and sip of wine is a Eucharist, a remembrance, a call to awareness of holiness right where we are..." —Shauna Niequist

Celebrating bread and wine is a daily delight for my husband and me. We savor the life-giving attributes of both in the sensory experience of sight, aroma, and taste—a taste of heaven—a foretaste of the feast to come.

What Would Jesus Pair?

In Christianity, bread became one of the most significant symbols of the faith. It was considered a miracle, a divine gift, a symbol of generosity, sharing, and hospitality, but mostly bread was a symbol of life. When Jesus taught the disciples to pray The Lord's Prayer (Mark 6:9-13), *"Our Father in heaven… Give us this day our daily bread…,"* it was a request for all that was needed to sustain life—physically and spiritually.

As manna, the bread sent from heaven, nourished and sustained the Israelites for forty years in the wilderness, so Jesus nourishes and sustains us spiritually as we journey through life on this side of heaven. Jesus is the new manna, the bread from heaven, and the only spiritual food we require—He is God's new covenant with His people.

Jesus comes from heaven, He is sent by the Father, He is the true bread that gives life to all who partake. *"Your fathers ate the manna in the wilderness, and they died. This is the bread that comes down from heaven, so that one may eat of it and not die. I am the living bread that came down from heaven. If anyone eats of this bread, he will live forever. And the bread that I will give for the life of the world is my flesh."*—John 6:49-51

Jesus was born in Bethlehem, is it a coincidence that the name Bethlehem means House of Bread? There are no coincidences with God. There is no life without bread—Bread is God's love made tangible through His Son Jesus.

5

FEASTS AND CELEBRATIONS

WHEN I WAS A CHILD my parents let me drink wine. The shock of it! As context is essential, there's a perspective that takes the shame out of it. I grew up in a traditional family, my mother was a fabulous, classic cook and Sunday dinners were a bit more formal and usually served in the dining room around a nicely laid table (instead of the everyday kitchen table). Our family nearly always ate dinner together. Even though we participated in activities and sports, most of the time dinnertime was spent together and uninterrupted. It wasn't like it is today. How was it that my parents knew that by sharing dinnertime together they were providing the essential time for the benefit of our family? We were far from the idealized "Cleavers," but we had our moments.

My father had been fighter pilot in the Air Force, and many years before I was born, he and my mother lived in Germany on air bases in wine country. They enjoyed the white wines of the Mosel region and *Zeller Schwarze Katz* became the Sunday offering at dinner when I was a child; it was served in special Mosel glasses with green stems.

Germany has a long history and love affair with wine and the shape and color of the bottle and stem of the glass used identifies the region. Green glass is indicative of a wine hailing from the Mosel region, and amber is representative of the Rhine. My father ordered Mosel wine by the case, and my sisters and I were treated to a small (very small) taste of wine in a very special Mosel glass on Sundays. As a result, the meal was elevated to a celebrated event.

Was my parents' sense of the importance of family dinner, especially Sunday dinner, part of their cognitive thinking? Or do we, as humans, have an innate proclivity to share and celebrate the meal? The ones that are the most memorable are those shared with family and friends, not the ones we have alone. It's always special to have dinner with others even when there is no special occasion. Food is essential for survival, but the social meal raises it to a new level—an occasion to celebrate the good gifts of creation—and it began in the Garden of Eden filled with culinary delights. The Jews believe that the Sabbath was established at creation; it is a day for the family and friends to spend time together, to rest and reflect.

Creating community and celebrating God's blessings while eating a meal together is at the heart of ancient banquets and feasts. The New Testament reveals many stories about Jesus attending celebrations that centered around food and wine and they include the weekly Sabbath meal, the Passover Seder, weddings, harvest celebrations, and other religious feasts. Jesus tells His disciples and the Pharisees a parable of a father who had two sons, the second one asked for his inheritance and promptly squandered it. Returning in shame with a repentant heart, the loving father subsequently celebrated the homecoming of his wayward son (much to the chagrin of his older brother) with a lavish feast. They killed the *fatted calf* (Luke 15:11-32).

> *But the father said to is servants, 'Bring the best robe, and put it on him, and put a ring on his hand, and shoes on his feet. And bring the fatted calf and kill it, and let us eat and celebrate. For this my son was dead, and is alive again; he was lost, and is found,' And they began to celebrate.* —Luke 15:22-24

You can count on the fact that there was plenty of food—especially bread and wine—at this homecoming celebration as with all ancient feasts and banquets. Even then, the bread and wine pointed to a much greater significance; the father in the parable welcomed home his lost son to a lavish supper, and our Savior Jesus welcomes us to His table, The Lord's Supper. Grace, mercy, and restoration are at the heart of such a banquet.

Drinking and Eating Together

One of the Hebrew nouns for feasts and banquets (*mišteh*) is derived from the Hebrew verb for drinking (*šātâ*). Its etymology parallels the Greek prefix *sun* ("with" or "together") and the verb *pino* ("to drink"). The Passover meal is a wonderful example of how feasting and drinking are intertwined in Jewish life.

As part of the Passover Seder, there are four cups of wine, known in Hebrew as arba kosot, and they are drunk by each participant at the Passover Seder service. In addition to the blessing of the four cups of wine, the Seder includes the breaking of the bread (matzah) and the subsequent blessing of the bread. The meal is meant to be reverent, but not solemn—it is a time of joy. After all the ritual observances in the Seder, a small feast begins. In ancient times, meat was considered too extravagant for the Sabbath meal and served primarily on the three more important feast days of the year.

Rob and I have thrown numerous dinner parties and winemaker events in all the years we have been together. Every detail from soup to nuts has been planned with care. The table is properly set with pressed linens, cloth napkins, polished silverware, and especially a lot of high-quality wine glasses. My husband's motto is, *"You can't have too many glasses on the table."* I spend a great deal of time planning the menu and the wine pairings, shopping for the best ingredients, and the house is thoroughly cleaned. Finally, the candles are lit, and mood music is piped through the speakers as the guests arrive to a celebratory glass of Champagne and hors d' oeuvres while the wine decants. The meal commences, and we ultimately linger over the wine as conversation ensues. Once the evening comes to an end, despite the mounds of dishes, there's a sense of satisfaction in knowing our gathering was a success.

First-Century Feasts

Our party prep and planning are not a new phenomenon. This scenario dates to ancient history. The event, whatever it might have been, was an opportunity to gather together and share all the gifts of nature—and at the heart of it was the food and wine. Hospitality was then and still is now an important gesture as hosts joyfully receive their guests and serve them generously according to the traditions. There's an added incentive: *"Do not neglect to show hospitality to strangers, for thereby some have entertained angels unawares"* (Hebrews 13:2). You never know who's coming to dinner.

There is some commonality in the social practices among the Mediterranean and Near Eastern cultures in the time of Jesus despite their religious differences. This is due to the fact that they were all initially conquered by the Greeks and then by the Romans. One could recognize similarities in certain practices such as written invitations, and customs during the banquet like hymn singing and reciting of prayers. Guests were honored to be invited and dressed for the occasion, they often used perfume and oils for these special times. Having been similarly occupied by the Greeks and Romans, these countries had the opportunity to share in certain cultural hospitality practices which became ingrained in their customs.

While there remained distinctions between many of the social and religious customs of these regions, their respective cuisine shared certain ingredients. The dietary patterns in flavors and staples like flatbreads, roasted meats, fruits, vegetables, olives, and olive oil were in some ways universal. Of course, the geography provided some limitations—obtaining fish in the desert would have been problematic unless you were on the Sea of Galilee. They all used condiments like wine, vinegar, honey, salt, and broth. And not surprisingly, bread and wine were central to nearly every meal.

The social aspect and intent of the banquet or feast played into the number of people who were invited. Weddings were the best of celebrations and as we will explore further, typically lasted up to a week and included throngs of people—in Hebrew, it's called a *simcha* (a joyous occasion). But, for banquets, a Greco-Roman host would have taken into consideration the size of the room and weighed the sense of community and atmosphere they wished to extend to their guests. Too many people would not be conducive to conversation unless people broke off into smaller groups, but with a smaller group, they could share in the same conversation.

> *Jesus, knowing that the Father had given all things into his hands, and that he had come from God and was going back to God, rose from supper. He laid aside his outer garments, and taking a towel, tied it around his waist. Then he poured water into a basin and began to wash the disciples' feet and to wipe them with the towel that was wrapped around him.* —John 13:3-5

For the formal Greek and Roman banquet, guests were received in an anteroom. Servants would wash their feet and use perfumed oil. Although this resembles a modern-day spa treatment, it was done for practical purposes. People walked in sandals on the dusty, dirty roads, so it was essential that their feet be washed before a meal, especially since people reclined at a low table and feet were exposed while eating.

We see Jesus, as described in the Gospel of John, performing this lowly task—the task of a servant—for His disciples at the Last Supper. For Jesus, it was the display of His humility and His servanthood. It was also for the benefit of the disciples. Jesus washing their feet was in contrast with their attitudes at that time—they had been arguing as to who was the greatest among them. Impetuous Peter was opposed to his teacher taking this posture, of course he was, but Jesus was illustrating the character that should be at the heart the true follower—to serve and not be served.

Interestingly, the guests at most banquets of the time were all men and conversation would have typically revolved around politics, religion, and philosophy. The exception was that certain feasts and religious festivals would have naturally included women, their wives.

The formal meal occurred in a luxurious setting for the wealthy, and the first part of all feasts began similarly to modern day practices, with a blessing—a prayer of thanksgiving for the bread: *Blessed are you, Lord, our God, King of the Universe who brings forth bread from the earth.* The host provided the best food and wine that they could afford and hospitality was a religion in itself. This custom predates Jesus by about 1,800 years as seen when Scripture recounts the time that Abraham and Sarah prepared a feast for three strangers (Genesis 18:1-8). The three strangers turned out to be angels—they entertained angels unaware, and Abraham knew he was in the presence of the Lord.

In addition to quantities of bread, the feast consisted of vegetables like lettuce, onions, and leeks, beans, herbs, and olives. Cheese and dairy products were also important to the meal, and sometimes fish and fowl (doves and pigeons) were included. Only lavish feasts included meat. As you can imagine, fish was popular in the Mediterranean regions as well as in communities around the Sea of Galilee. Lamb and goat were the likely choice of meat if provided, as well as some beef and pork for non-Jews.

The second part of the luxurious feasts of the time was known as the symposium. After the main meal, the tables were cleared, floors swept, and a new table was laid. Fresh and dried fruit, pistachios, almonds, hard boiled eggs, and sweet cakes with honey were presented. The focus of the evening shifted to entertainment and wine—the wine was mixed with water in a common bowl known as a krater. A prayer of thanksgiving for the wine was lifted up; *Blessed are You, Lord, our God, King of the Universe, who created the fruit of the vine.*

> *There was a practice at Greek banquets that the first taste of wine during the symposium came from a common cup. After the blessing, a small amount of wine was poured from the cup into the fire or onto the floor as an offering of thanksgiving. The host then offered a simple thanksgiving, drank from the cup and passed it to the next guest. Each guest at the banquet did the same. After the guest drank from the common cup, each individual cup was filled from the common bowl.* —Douglas E. Neel, and Joel A. Pugh, *The Food and Feasts of Jesus*

Was this a common practice for the Jews of the time of Jesus? Probably yes. This certainly resembles the cup that was shared in the upper room among the disciples at the

Last Supper and mimics the Christian church's practice of communion... *"for this is my blood of the covenant, which is poured out for many for the forgiveness of sins"* (Matthew 26:28).

Banquets and feasts were highly revered events in the first century as they are today. I truly believe that since the beginning of time, we have been imbued with an innate proclivity to share and celebrate the meal in fellowship with one another. The meals that are the most memorable are the ones shared with family and friends—new and old. Our modern-day Thanksgiving feast is a good example of how time-treasured traditions celebrated with those we are the closest is necessary for our spiritual survival. During the recent pandemic, when we experienced isolation, the lack of *community* had near devastating effects.

The feasts and banquets, the wedding celebrations, the Passover Seder, and the Communion of our Lord all point us to the Feast of the Lamb that will be celebrated together in the Father's Kingdom—in heaven. It's no coincidence that Jesus' last meal, The Last Supper, was a banquet in the company of His chosen disciples with the bread and wine as a central focus signifying His body and blood.

> *The cup of blessing that we bless, is it not a participation in the blood of Christ? The bread that we break, is it not a participation in the body of Christ?*
> —1 Corinthians 10:16

6

Blessed Generations

My mother's family tree is something that eluded her for the first sixty-five years of her life. At a certain point, she simply had to know where she came from. She knew her father came from the Black Forest region in Germany, and her stepmother was from New Jersey. But there was a big void about her mother who was orphaned at nine, raised in a Catholic orphanage in Germany, and died giving birth to her. She was told of her mother's family that there was nobody—no family. Every person has a family line, and she knew there had to be someone out there. After twenty-six years of searching she found them. My father swears that it was an angel, who one night out in cyberspace, led him to Mom's relatives, and then she disappeared.

That one email opened a whole world for our family. It turned out the statement made that there was nobody was untrue, because there were a lot of them—a big clan in Germany—and we all became close. The first thing we did when they came to visit was to open a bottle of German wine to celebrate with a big German dinner (my mother's specialty). And the first thing they did when

What Would Jesus Pair?

we went to visit them was... open a bottle of German wine and prepare a big German meal. Any time I drink German wine, I secretly thank God for my roots and wonderful big family. An appreciation of wine was in our history, it was the wine of the Mosel region that my family always enjoyed—and the first wine region established in Germany. It was in our blood; it was our heritage.

Jesus had a heritage. He was an ordinary carpenter from the town of Nazareth in Galilee whose life made an extraordinary impact on the world. What we know about Jesus is mostly from the last three years of His life—His life of ministry. We don't think of Jesus as a family guy playing with his siblings and sharing meals. Many people aren't even aware that Jesus had siblings. He did. Matthew 13:55 and Mark 6:3 name four men called Jesus' brothers: James, Joses (short for Joseph, Jr.), Simon, and Judas called Jude. Verse 56 mentions that Jesus had sisters. The sisters are not named, but since the word is plural there were at least two of them. Could you imagine having Jesus as your brother? I could hear Mary and Joseph say to His siblings, *"Why can't you be more like Jesus?"*

And what of His earthly mother and father? Mary is said to descend on her father's side from the tribe of Judah, and on her mother's from the tribe of Levi. Joseph descended from David through his son, Solomon. For such common people, there was something special, and in some instances royal, in their family tree.

A Return to Nazareth

> *He went away from there and came to his hometown, and his disciples followed him. And on the Sabbath he began to teach in the synagogue, and many who heard him were astonished, saying, "Where did this man get these things? What is the wisdom given to him? How are such mighty works done by his hands? Is not this the carpenter, the son of Mary and brother of James and Joses and Judas and Simon?* —Mark 6:1-3

It makes me wonder what kind of celebration they had in the neighborhood when Jesus arrived—especially having heard of His mighty works healing the sick, raising the dead, and turning water into wine. He would have been the hometown hero without question. Surely there were festivities planned in His honor. Did they prepare a feast for the occasion? And what's a feast without wine? Was there even wine to be had in Nazareth?

We know there was no such celebration as the people in Nazareth were unwilling to accept Jesus' teachings because they looked at Him as one of them, a commoner with whom they grew up—He was not thought to be anyone special, *"Can anything good come out of Nazareth?"* (John 1:46). So, after a few healings, He and the disciples left. No celebration feast, no party, no wine. This astounds me.

Had there been a celebration there would have been special food and wine included on the menu, perhaps even their best wine. A recent, twenty-first century discovery in Nazareth Village provides evidence of winemaking in the region. Archeologists found a 2,000-year-old winepress that was hewn out of the bedrock. Such small presses were common features in the Hellenistic and Early Roman periods. But the location of this winepress—just 500 meters from the original village of Nazareth—makes it very significant. Jesus grew up drinking locally made wine with His family. Wine was a common beverage of the day, and safer to drink than water.

Matthew Speaks into the Silence

The very first book of the New Testament was authored by Matthew. Four hundred tumultuous years had lapsed since the Old Testament ended and it was a time of biblical silence. Matthew was one of the twelve disciples called by Jesus; he was a despised tax collector, and he was likely the most notorious of sinners among them. He, along with ten of the twelve, was from Galilee, a predominantly rural region of small towns and villages. As for their station in life? Well, they were not exactly considered anything special, they were commoners—fishermen and farmers.

Matthew, very intentionally, begins his Gospel message with the genealogy of Jesus before he gets into

His birth. At first it seemed odd to me that this Gospel (and the entire New Testament) starts off with a list of names. In many ways, however, this is the best introduction to the New Testament. The family tree of Jesus reflects the Jewish hope anchored in His roots—the Jews were promised a child from the family of Israel. The 400 years since the Old Testament went dark opens with the story of the prophesied Messiah. Matthew shows us God's story is not a fairy tale. This is the true story of the Son of God who has a family tree on earth and was born in the line of King David, nonetheless.

Matthew begins by calling Jesus the son of David, pointing to His royal origin, and also the son of Abraham, indicating that He was an Israelite. In both instances, calling Jesus "son" means He was a descendant. It clearly reflects the promises God made to David (Israel's second king) and to Abraham (the father of the nation).

Genealogy of Jesus Christ

The book of the genealogy of Jesus Christ, the son of David, the son of Abraham. Abraham was the father of Isaac, and Isaac the father of Jacob, and Jacob the father of Judah and his brothers ... and Jesse the father of David the king. —Matthew 1:1-2, 6

What Would Jesus Pair?

God refers to Himself as the God of Abraham, Isaac, and Jacob about a dozen times throughout both the Old and New Testaments. This name of God emphasizes the covenant that He made with Israel. The Israelites hold a special place as God's Chosen People.

Matthew wastes no time emphasizing the fact that Jesus is from the line of Abraham and lays out the entire lineage of forty-two descendants between the two. In Genesis, God told Abraham to leave his home and travel to Canaan. He then promised the land of Canaan to Abraham's descendants. But Abraham was seventy-five years old and didn't have a son at the time. Later, he and his wife, Sarah, gave birth to Isaac when they were nearly 100 years old, making him truly the father of the nation as God had promised.

Through Isaac, Jacob was born, and God gave him the new name Israel. In the Old Testament, vineyards represented the chosen people, Israel. Why is Israel called Israel? Abraham's descendants were enslaved by the Egyptians for hundreds of years before settling in Canaan (a blessed land of wine and wheat), which is approximately the region of modern-day Israel and still recognized for their vineyards and wine. The word, Israel, comes from Abraham's grandson, Jacob.

From Jacob came the Twelve Tribes of Israel, and eventually, Jesus. Through Abraham the nation of Israel was born, as well as their promised Messiah. These were truly blessed generations.

But what does this all have to do with wine? Wine (and bread) played an important role in the blessings we see throughout the first descendants of this lineage of Christ. When God promised His people the land of Canaan, He spoke of blessings, *"And I will make of you a great nation, and I will bless you and make your name great, so that you will be a blessing. I will bless those who bless you, and him who dishonors you I will curse, and in you all the families of the earth shall be blessed"* (Genesis 12:2-3). It was something they could look forward to in the Promised Land that would later be described as—a land of wheat and barley, of vines and fig trees and pomegranates, a land of olive trees and honey (Deuteronomy 8:8).

Abraham's journey, when he was called to leave his home in Ur for the land of Canaan, was a wine route of sorts. As he traveled to Shechem, he would have likely trekked through Imar, Ebla, Qata, and Damascus on his way. Ancient wine presses have been found in all of these places on that route; so needless to say, Abraham and his family drank the wine and ate the local food of these different regions.

While the biblical account of wine begins with Noah planting the first vineyard in Mount Ararat, it was through Abraham's journeys within the Fertile Crescent to Mesopotamia on His way to the Promised Land we begin to see the blessings unfold. This *promised* land had the best conditions for growing grapes and making wine. The richness of the land would have provided the best of the fruits of earth which are frequently referred to throughout Scripture.

The First Covenant Blessing

> *And Melchizedek king of Salem brought out bread and wine. (He was priest of God Most High) And he blessed him and said, "Blessed be Abram by God Most High, Possessor of heaven and earth; and blessed be God Most High, who has delivered your enemies into your hand!" And Abram gave him a tenth of everything.*
> —Genesis 14:18-20

Here, Melchizedek met Abraham (previously called Abram) on his victorious return from battle, gave him bread and wine and blessed him in the name of "God Most High" Interestingly, his name first means king of righteousness, that is, king of peace, then king of Salem. By all accounts, he is without a father, without a mother, and he has neither beginning days nor end of life—in this regard he is like the Son of God—and he remains a priest for all time.

> *So also Christ did not exalt himself to be made a high priest, but was appointed by him who said to him, "You*

are my Son, today I have begotten you"; as he says also in another place, "You are a priest forever, after the order of Melchizedek." —Hebrews 5:5-6

Why did Melchizedek choose to bless Abraham with bread and wine? Historically, bread and wine were often associated with covenant meals, and in this Genesis story we encounter the first covenant meal. The mention of Melchizedek's priesthood infers that he is not providing sustenance to Abraham because he didn't lack food, but rather, he lacked the righteousness, something Melchizedek inherently possessed. Some would suggest that this is a precursor of the Lord's Supper—the body and blood of Christ. Abraham being blessed by Melchizedek with bread and wine propitiously points to our redemption through a greater king of righteousness who will come from Abraham's line—Jesus Christ.

Later, Abraham was tested by God. God told him to sacrifice his only son, Isaac. He said, "Take your son, your only son Isaac, whom you love, and go to the land of Moriah, and offer him there as a burnt offering on one of the mountains of which I shall tell you."
—Genesis 22:2

Abraham obeyed. As a result of his obedience, Isaac was ultimately spared, and God blessed him. *"I will surely* bless you, and I will surely multiply your offspring as the stars of heaven and as the sand that is on the seashore. And your offspring shall possess the gate of his enemies, and in your offspring shall all the nations of the earth be blessed." —Genesis 22:17-18

Isaac Blesses the Next Generation

Then he said, "Bring it near to me, that I may eat of my son's game and bless you." So he brought it near to him, and he ate; and he brought him wine, and he drank. Then his father Isaac said to him, "Come near and kiss me, my son." So he came near and kissed him. And Isaac smelled the smell of his garments and blessed him and said, "See, the smell of my son is as the smell of a field that the Lord has blessed! May God give you of the dew of heaven and of the fatness of the earth and plenty of grain and wine. —Genesis 27:25-28

Isaac, before his death, was planning to bless Esau, his oldest son. Isaac's wife, Rebekah, learned of his plan and devised a plot whereby Jacob, the youngest son, would be blessed instead of the older son. She prepared a meal and told Jacob to carry it to Isaac who "was old and his eyes were so dim that he could not see" (Gen. 27:1). Jacob took the meal prepared by his mother to his father, a meal that included savory food, bread, and wine; and Isaac ate and drank.

Jacob received the covenant blessing from his father, albeit through trickery. The meal, as mentioned, specifically included bread and wine, reminding us of the first covenant blessing made by Melchizedek to his grandfather, Abraham. Esau was not happy and challenged his father, but Isaac made it clear that he had already given him the blessing, and along with it was his birthright. *Isaac answered and said to Esau, "Behold, I have made him lord over you, and all his brothers I have given to him for servants, and with grain and wine I have sustained him* (Genesis 27:36-37). Wine was the key element in sustaining the family blessing. Later, Jacob purchased land that fulfilled the blessing as he planted vineyards and grain fields.

> *Isaac's blessing of Jacob, who would later be named Israel, was symbolic of the profound place that wine held in the emerging Israelite religion as well as the cultural and economic significance of wine.* —Randall Hesket and Joel Butler, *Divine Vintage*

Abraham handed down his legacy of grape growing and winemaking practices through the generations onto Joseph. Jacob blessed Joseph: *"Joseph is a fruitful bough, a fruitful bough by a spring; his branches run over the wall"* (Genesis 49:22). We see in the story of Joseph, Jacob's son, a beautiful illustration of the subsequent saga of wine continuing to unfold. During Joseph's lifetime, Canaan was a prolific viticultural center.

Jacob was the father of the twelve sons whose families would become the twelve tribes of the nation. And later, God would give to the nation that came from the line of Jacob the blessing of the fruit of the vine—a blessing of wine.

Jacob's twelve sons became the twelve tribes of the nation. Two of his sons, Judah and Joseph, were greatly blessed as we see in the parallels between the two in that the descendants of each became the major tribes of Israel. Both Judah and Joseph prospered.

> *But most importantly, Jacob blessed Judah, in the line of Jesus with the kingship of Israel: "Judah, your brothers shall praise you; your hand shall be on the neck of your enemies; your father's sons shall bow down before you... The scepter shall not depart from Judah, nor the ruler's staff from between his feet until tribute comes to him; and to him shall be the obedience of the peoples. Binding his foal to the vine and his donkey's colt to the choice vine, he has washed his garments in wine and his vesture in the blood of grapes. His eyes are darker than wine, and his teeth whiter than milk."* —Genesis 49:8,10-12

Jesus, forty-two generations later, fulfilled the covenant blessing through bread and wine that was first given to His ancestor, Abraham, and it became the *new* covenant 1,800 years later.

> *There shall come forth a shoot from the stump of Jesse, and a branch from his roots shall bear fruit.*
> —Isaiah 11:1

Can anything good come from Nazareth? Jesus, the One True Vine, whose branches bear fruit, sprang from a family of blessed generations. Jesus, the shoot from the stump of Jesse, from the line of Abraham, Isaac, Jacob, and Judah changed the world forever.

I was able to discover a lot about my family genealogy. And while we are mostly a line of ordinary people, I have come to realize it doesn't matter because we are the branches of the True Vine. God blessed my family with vineyards and wine through which we have been transformed—and for that we too are grateful.

Section II

Food and wine take center stage in many biblical accounts of Jesus and His ancestors. The curtain opens at the beginning of time in a lush garden and continues through the New Testament with these selected stories and suggested dishes accompanied by recipes that highlight each one with a modern take.

7

A Garden of Eden

And God said, "Let the earth sprout vegetation, plants yielding seed, and fruit trees bearing fruit in which is their seed, each according to its kind, on the earth." And it was so. And God saw that it was good.
—Genesis 1:11, 12

I GREW UP IN NEW Jersey. What many people don't realize is that New Jersey is appropriately nicknamed The Garden State. Farming and agriculture are still dominant; you simply cannot get a better tasting tomato than the Jersey tomato. Someone fittingly suggested that they change to a new nickname—The Tomato State. Roadside stands feature tomatoes, white and yellow Jersey corn, fresh fruits, and vegetables, and the cranberry bogs are a sight to see. I grew up with local dairy-fresh milk delivered to our home, and we passed farms on our way to school just a few miles away even though we lived in the suburbs. When I initially moved to Southern California, I enjoyed a different variety of fruits and vegetables that were not as readily available in my previous home state.

One of the most intriguing fruits I encountered was yellow fleshed watermelon. The yard of our first home in Orange County was a veritable Garden of Eden planted with apricots, persimmons, lemons, limes, and grapefruits; on one side, a hedge of boysenberries lined the entire length of our property. A huge jacaranda tree stood in the center of the yard profuse with purple blooms; palms, tropical bougainvillea, and exotic bird of paradise formed a natural hedge on the other side. We were in our own heaven.

The apricots were so plentiful that we couldn't eat them fast enough so we resorted to making our own apricot brandy; the same happy predicament applied to our boysenberries. Perhaps this was an unwitting precursor to our winemaking days. Persimmons—what are persimmons and what do you do with them? We had never tasted the likes of these rare fruits, and were fortunate that friends shared recipes for cookies, and sweet breads made from their unusual flesh.

Frequenting local farmer's markets became a ritual for us when we moved up to the Central Coast. Every Saturday morning, we would head to the village square in the quaint town of Templeton with our wagon and bags to haul home a carefully selected bounty of culinary treats. My boys especially loved sampling the strawberries, plums, and dates. The *Farm to Table* movement had become popular and was celebrated in the culinary community. We continued our tradition when we moved to Nebraska; within our first few days of living in Lincoln, we visited the large downtown market and shortly thereafter became acquainted with the locals who represented their locally grown, fresh produce and wares.

My oldest son, Spencer, planted 150 square feet of vegetable gardens in our new backyard, and my men wasted no time building a chicken coop. Alec has always loved his chickens. While we no longer need to rely on our own volition for food, there is something that is grounding when you dig into the dirt and work with the soil to grow your own produce and collect fresh eggs.

Drinking the wine that was produced from the grapes in our own vineyards in California seemed to taste better. The terroir—that certain sense of place—had become part of who we were, and we could taste it. The grapevines at harvest were lush and beautiful, and the grapes were delicious. Wine grapes are actually sweeter than table grapes making them perfect for fermenting.

And God said, "Behold, I have given you every plant yielding seed that is on the face of all the earth, and every tree with seed in its fruit. You shall have them for food. And God saw everything that he had made, and behold, it was very good. —Genesis 1:29, 31

What Would Jesus Pair?

Can you imagine what it was like for Adam and Eve to live in the Garden of Eden? Biblical history begins with the first man and woman in a lush garden eating fruit—and one forbidden fruit. Food is God's gift to humankind. And certainly, humans couldn't live long without it. As we have seen with manna, the bread from heaven, food plays a role in providing more than just physical sustenance. Maybe that's why God used an apple as the forbidden fruit. Truth be told, the Hebrew Bible doesn't say what kind of fruit it was. Scholars say it was definitely not an apple and speculate that it was a pomegranate, a grape, or even a fig—the couple did cover themselves modestly with fig leaves. Whatever it was, it was pleasing to the eye.

> *And out of the ground the Lord God made to spring up every tree that is pleasant to the sight and good for food.*
> —Genesis 2:9

What kind of fruits and vegetables did Adam and Eve eat? No one knows for certain, but knowledge of the geography of Eden would give us a good indication as to what fruits and vegetables would grow viably in the region—fruit and plants with seeds. The location of Eden is described in the Book of Genesis as the source of four tributaries. "*A river flowed out of Eden to water the garden, and there it divided and became four rivers*" (Genesis 2:10). Those rivers would likely be the Pishon, Gichon, Chidekel

(Tigris), and Perat (Euphrates). But the problem is that there is no central location from which all of these four rivers flow.

The Pishon is assumed to be the Nile River, and the Gichon the Blue Nile; they are both located in the southwest region, while the Euphrates and the Tigris are in the northeast region. This makes it difficult to determine the exact location of The Garden, but scholars can surmise that it is somewhere between the two.

Based on Genesis 2:10, there is a good chance that it might be located at the head of the Persian Gulf in southern Mesopotamia, which is now Iraq. If we look at what kinds of fruits and vegetables are grown in this region today, known as the fertile crescent (the fertile land watered by the Tigris and Euphrates), we see a similar variety that is mentioned in Scripture in the Holy Land—the land of plenty: onion, okra, eggplant, green bean, sweet pepper, squash, lettuce, spinach, chard, carrot, cabbage and cauliflower are some of the main vegetables, and date palm, citrus, grape, pomegranate, stone fruits (apricot, plum, peach, almond), pear, cucumber, watermelon, sweet melon, olive, and fig... are the main fruits. Also, readily available still today is barley, wheat, sesame, and flax.

The Bible tells us that the Garden of Eden was the earthly paradise created by God where He placed his first human creation. The word Eden is probably derived from the Akkadians, Akkad was the first ancient empire of

Mesopotamia—the Akkadian term *edinnu* means "plain". It is also closely related to an Aramaic root word, *edin*, meaning "fruitful, and well-watered." The Vulgate, which is the predominant Latin version of the Bible prepared in the late fourth century, refers to Eden as "paradisum voluptatis," or in English, "the paradise of pleasure".

The Douay-Rheims Catholic Bible describes Genesis 2:8 like this: *"And the Lord God had planted a paradise of pleasure from the beginning: wherein he placed man whom he had formed."*

Regardless of where the Garden of Eden is actually located, we know from Scripture that it is a paradise lush with colorful, edible plants that were pleasing in every way. God took pleasure in His creation and wanted Adam and Eve, His first humans, to take pleasure in it, but they blew it. Sometimes I wonder if this garden of paradise (after the fall) is much like that of heaven—too glorious for us to grasp this side of eternity. Perhaps it remains shrouded in mystery for a reason.

God doesn't make mistakes, I have to believe that He knew His creation would be tempted by something so very perfect, albeit forbidden, and fall into sin; we would eventually long for restoration with Him. Sometimes you have to lose something before you realize its true worth. God continually gives us glimpses of heaven and glimpses of the garden to remind us that He is *the* creator of all. This gives us a desire that drives us closer to Him—the

A Garden of Eden

Alpha and the Omega—from the beginning in the garden to the end in the eternity of heaven. It's so beautiful that we cannot even grasp it. Maybe this is why the garden is sometimes called the "Garden of God." Like heaven, it's beyond our comprehension.

I love to cook. When it comes to shopping for ingredients, it's the produce that takes most of my time to select as I revel in all the variety. When I am fortunate enough to harvest from our own vegetable and herb gardens, I am in my own sort of heaven. The color that fresh produce adds to a dish makes it more appetizing. Have you ever heard of eating the rainbow? It means that it's best if you choose a variety of different-colored fruits and vegetables every day. Respectively, the range of pigments in whole foods provide an assortment of much needed nutrients. Isn't it like God to use the rainbow, a symbol of His promise, to nourish His creation.

There is no limit as to what you can do with fruits and vegetables. I have cookbooks solely dedicated to both and enjoy creating something delicious and new. One of my favorites is by Alice Waters, who in the 1970s opened her restaurant, Chez Panisse, famous for its role in creating the farm-to-table movement and for pioneering California cuisine. She describes how she delights in her backyard garden and shares experiences of extraordinary farmers and chefs with their collective knowledge that has made this movement so prolific. She mentions that among the

What Would Jesus Pair?

many passions of Thomas Jefferson, one of them was for his garden and he was considered a farmer-gastronome. He planned his garden for pleasure and for the table, he had an adventurous palate and profound respect for agrarian values. This intrigued me.

I always thought my son, Spencer, would go into agriculture; since he was a little guy, if it had a seed, he wanted to grow it. Still to this day as a young adult, he has jars of all sizes with something growing from a seed in our kitchen—even a small fig tree. He dreams of what he will plant next and what recipe to conjure up from the produce harvested in his own Garden of Eden. Upon filling his basket to the brim with a beautiful variety, we all have fun laying out the colorful bounty across the countertop in a picture-perfect array, snapping photos, anticipating the scrumptious culinary delight that will be on the dinner menu. It's always an adventure and it is always good.

> *And God said, "Let the earth sprout vegetation, plants yielding seed, and fruit trees bearing fruit in which is their seed, each according to its kind, on the earth." And it was so. And God saw that it was good.*
>
> —Genesis 1:11, 12

The following suggested recipes celebrate the fruit of the Garden of Eden.

A Garden of Eden

- Charoset Salad (Charoset is a sweet, chunky, apple relish served at Passover), page 290
- Cantaloupe Melon Salad with Cucumber and Feta, page 291
- Fruited Israeli Couscous (warm dish), page 296

8

BARTERED FOR A BOWL OF STEW

When the boys grew up, Esau was a skillful hunter, a man of the field, while Jacob was a quiet man, dwelling in tents. Isaac loved Esau because he ate of his game, but Rebekah loved Jacob. —Genesis 25:27-28

NEW BEGINNINGS ARE GOOD FOR my soul. The beginning of summer brings some relief from the busy end of spring culminating in graduations, parties, and finally a chance to be a little more laid back for a while. The start of the school year brings excitement with new goals while jumping back into a much-needed routine. I always look forward to the milder, autumnal weather, the colorful landscape, and the aroma of pumpkin spice which is all so comforting. But when the calendar changes over to a new year, some people look at it as the most important new beginning of all with celebrations and resolutions.

As the new year arrives, we are once again reacquainted with the culinary traditions of cultures around the world. Hoping for prosperity and good fortune in the New Year is universal and celebrated with food. The Spanish eat

What Would Jesus Pair?

twelve grapes at the twelve strokes of midnight; in Mexico tamales are featured; sweet, ripened pomegranates are smashed on doorways in Turkey; marzipan pigs and pork are a German must have, lentils in Italy are simmered and served up, and in Scotland they drink Scotch—of course they do.

My in-laws always have pork and sauerkraut on New Year's Day, as does my family—only prepared differently and accompanied with lentils. Lentils are my families' favorite. My sisters prepare lentils in a number of ways, and it seems that every time I speak to my mother, she is making a pot of lentil soup. Her recipe is provided for you in the recipe section to try yourself (Mimi's Lentil Soup).

Lentils have been around since the beginning of time. The oldest written recipe for these particular legumes was found in Egypt and written in Greek. They are easy to grow, easy to prepare, very nutritious, and economical—they are considered a poor man's food. Along with the Egyptians, the ancient Romans and Hebrews commonly ate lentils, which are mentioned several times in the Bible. Genesis features the most notable story of a birthright being bartered for a bowl of stew—red lentil stew.

> *Once when Jacob was cooking stew, Esau came in from the field, and he was exhausted. And Esau said to Jacob, "Let me eat some of that red stew, for I am exhausted!" (Therefore his name was called Edom.) Jacob said, "Sell*

BARTERED FOR A BOWL OF STEW

> *me your birthright now." Esau said, "I am about to die; of what use is a birthright to me?" Jacob said, "Swear to me now." So he swore to him and sold his birthright to Jacob. Then Jacob gave Esau bread and lentil stew, and he ate and drank and rose and went his way.*
>
> —Genesis 25:29-34

Jacob is an interesting figure in biblical history. He is known for his restless faith and his wanderings, which ultimately brings him back to the Promised Land where he is buried with Abraham and Sarah, Isaac and Rebekah, and His wife, Leah. Jacob even wrestled with God (Genesis 32:22-32). He was the son of Isaac, and in comparison, did well for himself, but his worldly achievements were nothing to write home about. While he was not one of the greatest men in the Old Testament, he left a mark on history for which he rarely receives credit.

But what does this all have to do with Jesus?

Jacob fits into God's bigger plan. As we see at the opening of the Gospel of Matthew, Jesus' lineage is a big deal in the Bible. Most people are surprised when they find out it reaches back to Jacob (Jacob, the guy who stole his birthright for a bowl of stew). My husband always joked that he was reluctant to dig into his own genealogy because he was afraid his history includes a bunch of horse thieves. Contrary to his concern, he has a respectable lineage back to the founding of our nation, but he's convinced there's a horse thief in there somewhere.

Jesus was related to Jacob—the thief who tricked his twin brother out of his inheritance for lentil soup and bread. The story of Jacob spans twenty-five chapters of Genesis. But the highlight of his story is that he had twelve sons and they became the twelve tribes of Israel. Jacob had received a new name, Israel, which means the one who struggled with God and lived, and that is why his descendants became known as the Israelites. Some people also associate the meaning of the name with the country of Israel—the land of wheat and wine. Only two of the twelve tribes survived, Judah and Benjamin.

> *Taking one of the stones of the place, he put it under his head and lay down in that place to sleep. And he dreamed, and behold, there was a ladder set up on the earth, and the top of it reached to heaven. And behold, the angels of God were ascending and descending on it! And behold, the Lord stood above it and said, "I am the Lord, the God of Abraham your father and the God of Isaac."* —Genesis 28:11-13

In my sons' Action Bible (a graphic Bible), the illustrations of Jacob's Ladder are intriguing. They depict the prophetic dream in which Jacob sees a stairway-like ladder stretching from heaven to earth and angels going up and down. The dream represented the connection between God and man, but also that from his lineage, the nation of Israel, God's chosen people, would be born—the numerous offspring would prove to be the blessing of the entire Earth. Out of the line of Jacob came the promised Messiah, God's only Son, Jesus. (Matthew 1:1-17). Jesus is from the line of Judah; the symbol of the tribe is a lion—Jesus is the Lion of Judah.

> *Then Jacob awoke from his sleep and said, "Surely the Lord is in this place, and I did not know it." And he was afraid and said, "How awesome is this place! This is none other than the house of God, and this is the gate of heaven." So early in the morning Jacob took the stone that he had put under his head and set it up for a pillar and poured oil on the top of it. He called the name of that place Bethel.* —Genesis 28:16-19

As the story of the Exodus reveals God's physical and spiritual provision with the gift of manna, so does the feeding of the 5,000 through bread and fish, the wedding at Cana with water turned into wine, and even Elijah was fed bread and meat by the ravens in the wilderness. We see Jacob's story, which stretched back 1,800 years before the birth of Jesus, as one that centers around food, however with an interesting twist—the food nourished Esau physically, but paved the way, through Jacob, for God's chosen

What Would Jesus Pair?

people to be nourished spiritually by his descendent, Jesus. And it all started with a bowl of red lentil stew.

Providing food that nourishes body and soul is an ageless desire in all cultures. Food is a language of love and not surprisingly the subject of many books and cookbooks. It reminds me of a particular cold and rainy day when we lived in California and were bottling one of our wines along with other wineries. We were first in the bottling line and once our wine was finished, I could tell it was going to be a long, chilly day for everyone else. I told the crew I'd be back with a warm treat to go with the sandwiches that were ordered.

With what I could scrounge from my cupboard and refrigerator, I started chopping vegetables and simmering lentils for a large pot of soup. Before I was finished, my mother-in-law who was staying with us for a short while, pulled a spiral ham (drizzled with glaze) out of the oven to take to her card-club luncheon. I had divine inspiration. I used the reserved drippings infused with glaze and bits of ham trimmings to finish my soup. I was winging it but created the best lentil soup I had ever made. I took it back to the winery and I could tell that it not only warmed their bodies that were chilled to the bone, but it nourished their souls, and everyone was able to finish their tasks with a new spirit.

I can't remember what wine we paired with the soup—we were in a winery after all that was filled with

Bartered for a Bowl of Stew

barrels of vintages and varietals—but my winemaker, Rich, still talks about the best lentil soup ever.

Lentils have been around forever and were a common dish of the first century. Jesus surely ate lentils with plenty of bread and wine at Passover, the wedding at Cana, while dining with the Pharisees, and at most feasts and celebrations. Lentils might be considered a poor man's food that nourishes the body—but it is especially good for one's soul.

If you are willing and obedient, you shall eat the good of the land. —Isaiah 1:19

The following suggested recipes feature the versatility of lentils, from soup, to sides, and salads.

- Mimi's Lentil Soup (better than Jacob's Pottage), page 277
- Brown Butter Lentil and Sweet Potatoes Salad, page 288
- Roasted Beet Salad with Lentils and Goat Cheese, page 286

9

Saint Peter's Fish

And when he had finished speaking, he said to Simon, "Put out into the deep and let down your nets for a catch." And Simon answered, "Master, we toiled all night and took nothing! But at your word I will let down the nets." And when they had done this, they enclosed a large number of fish, and their nets were breaking.

—Luke 5:4-6

GROWING UP AND SPENDING OUR summers at the Jersey shore, we lived close to the water. We were within a quick jaunt to a tiny, bay beach, and as kids that was our favorite place in the whole world; we loved to go crabbing. There is nothing quite as scrumptious as freshly caught blue claws steamed to perfection and dipped in drawn butter, and now as an adult with a slightly chilled glass of Chardonnay. We usually caught our crabs with a line and sinker threaded with bunker-fish bait dropped into the water and slowly pulled up when there was a tug on our line, a task which requires patience and skill.

What Would Jesus Pair?

Hanging over the side of a boat, or off the pier, we'd test our luck—we were usually pretty lucky.

My sister and best friend, Missy, and I loved to watch other people drag their seining nets out from the water onto the shore. Their haul usually included a veritable treasure trove of sea creatures including crabs. Oftentimes these *fishermen* were not interested in the crabs, but instead fish—little bait fish. It was fun to watch the shiny, silver fish jumping in the nets on the sand. Sometimes, they came up empty handed, and sometimes they'd have an impressive haul—but nothing like that of the disciples when Jesus commanded them to put down their nets.

The disciples had been fishing all night and were nearing the shore empty handed. They were tired and hungry. But Jesus changed all of that. Not only did He provide plenty, He provided more than enough—does this story of abundance sound familiar? As the heavy, brimming nets were hauled in, Jesus, after being resurrected, appeared for the third time to His disciples and was there on the beach waiting for them.

> *When they got out on land, they saw a charcoal fire in place, with fish laid out on it, and bread. Jesus said to them, "Bring some of the fish that you have just caught." Jesus said to them, "Come and have breakfast."*
>
> —John 21:9-10, 12

Jesus cooked them breakfast and they broke bread together over their fish. This miracle of such an extraordinary catch, and of Jesus, having been resurrected and serving them, marks the awakening of faith that the disciples experienced in a profound way.

Two ordinary fishermen, Simon Peter and his brother Andrew, were the first among whom Jesus called to follow Him (Matthew 4:18-20). The livelihood of these initial disciples would be changed dramatically; they had been fishing out on the Sea of Galilee, but from that moment on they would be *fishers of men* out in the world.

My husband and I spent our tenth anniversary in Croatia; we were invited by our friend who had a villa in Dubrovnik on the Adriatic Sea. It was nothing short of stunning. One day, after touring his hillside vineyards, we stopped for lunch and dined alfresco next to the sea. Croatian cuisine is influenced by the traditions of the Mediterranean, so as you could imagine, fish is a prominent dish that is frequently served. We were more than happy when our host offered to order for us. Out came the most beautiful, whole, fish grilled with coarse sea salt and herbs, presented with wedges of lemon and served with a glass of Maraština, a classic, Croatian white wine. A chef came to our table to delicately filet and plate our individual fish; it was a memorable experience. The fish was musht (tilapia) which is also known as St. Pierre or Peter's Fish.

What Would Jesus Pair?

This fish is the most prominent of the species still caught today in the Sea of Galilee. Peter, Andrew, and the other disciples were fishing for tilapia and that's how it got its nickname, St. Peter's fish. There is another fish that is attributed to Peter, The John Dory, which has dark spots on the sides of its body, referred to as *St. Peter's thumbprint*. Legend says that the spots were left by the apostle Peter as he was catching fish—truly a blessed fish—which explains another version of its nickname.

While I love bagels and lox with cream cheese for Sunday brunch, or better yet a heavily smoked filet of salmon with Hollandaise, the idea of fish for breakfast doesn't thrill me. Some cultures, however, serve fish for breakfast. My father, while flying for the Air Force, told us of the magnificent breakfast spreads in the officer's club in Stavanger, Norway that included a lot of fish.

Fish is not specifically mentioned as a breakfast item in the Bible, yet Jesus prepared the fish the disciples had caught as a side to the bread He was cooking over a fire (John 21:10-12). They were breaking bread together, but why would Jesus break from the norm by serving fish? All speculation points to the fact that the fish became an early Christian symbol, and Jesus never wasted a teaching moment—this one was prophetic. He had just performed a miracle for the benefit of His disciples. What Jesus was illustrating was clear—I will make you fishers of men. The fish was their symbol.

The Greek word for fish is "ichthys." As early as the first century, Christians made an acrostic from this word: *Iesous Christos Theou Yios Soter*—Jesus Christ, Son of God, Savior. The fish also has other theological overtones as well, Jesus fed the 5,000 with two fishes (St. Peter's fish nonetheless) and five loaves, and He called His disciples "fishers of men." Water baptism, practiced by immersion in the early church, created a parallel between fish and converts. The second-century theologian Tertullian said: "We, little fishes, after the image of our Ichthys, Jesus Christ, are born in the water."

The Greeks and Romans, as well as many pagans used the fish symbol before the Christians had. And as such, the fish didn't attract suspicion (unlike the symbol of the cross), making it a perfect secret symbol for persecuted believers. When threatened by Romans in the first centuries after Christ, Christians used the fish to mark meeting places and tombs, or to distinguish friends from foes. According to one ancient story, when a Christian met a stranger in the road, the Christian sometimes drew one arc of the simple fish outline in the dirt. If the stranger drew the other arc, both believers knew they were in good company.[2]

The symbol of the fish plays an important part in Judaic traditions as well. Many parables in the Torah

---

[2] ChristianityToday.com, "What is the origin of the Christian fish symbol? A closer look at the ancient Ichthys," by Elesha Coffman.

affiliate fish with the Jewish people. Fish was an important dietary supplement in the ancient world when it was available. Old Testament Scripture tells us that Jerusalem even had a marketplace called Fish Gate. Fish was consumed in a variety of ways including fresh cooked or raw, dried, salted, and pickled. The Jewish dietary laws divided fish into two categories, clean and unclean. Fish with scales and fins were considered clean, while shellfish were unclean.

Fish also provided other byproducts such as fish brine for cooking, fish oil for fuel, their skins were dried and used as a writing surface, and fishbones were fashioned into writing implements, hooks, needles, and hair ornaments. New Testament Scripture referred to the importance of fishing in the first century, so it's not surprising that Jesus would choose prominent fishermen, Peter, Andrew, James, and John among His first disciples.

While walking by the Sea of Galilee, he saw two brothers, Simon (who is called Peter) and Andrew his brother, casting a net into the sea, for they were fishermen. And he said to them, "Follow me, and I will make you fishers of men." Immediately they left their nets and followed him. —Matthew 4:18-20

My sons, Spencer and Alec, love to fish. My oldest, Spencer, lives to fish. The first thing they did when we moved into our new home, even before the boxes were completely unpacked, was to dig a large pond with their dad, and stock it with bass and catfish. I believe that if they lived in first-century Galilee, they would have been

Saint Peter's Fish

among those called by Jesus to follow Him. I am in awe of their love for the Lord, and their desire to live out their calling—they are truly *fishers of men.*

The following suggested recipes highlight the basics of timeless fish dishes.

- Whole Baked St. Peter's Fish (with four sauce variations), page 300
    - Lemon Cream Sauce, page 302
    - Green Goddess Sauce, page 303
    - Greek Ladolemono Sauce, page 304
    - Romesco Sauce, page 304
- Mediterranean Fish Stew, page 305

10

A Wedding At Cana

We take for granted the slow miracle whereby water in the irrigation of a vineyard becomes wine. It is only when Christ turns water into wine, in a quick motion, as it were, that we stand amazed. —Saint Augustine

WHEN WE LIVED ON A vineyard in the rolling hills of California wine country, in Paso Robles, the people who visited were in awe of this seeming paradise. And in some ways, it was—paradise. Our Mediterranean style home was perched atop a prominent hill visible from miles around. Massive windows and numerous French doors revealed stunning 360° views which stretched on as far as the eye could see. Elegant Cabernet grapevines wound their way up to the foot of our home and sprawled down into valleys and out of sight. Decks and balconies provided vistas much like that of a Tuscan villa. Classic mission olive trees, aromatic lavender, and perpetually blooming rosemary hedges set the backdrop of this enchanted setting.

Most of the vineyards and wineries in this viticultural paradise, big or boutique, modern or rustic, and everything in-between were similar to ours in one way or another. And they provided the perfect setting for a party. We were guests at many of these classic venues for various celebrations; there was always a reason to celebrate in wine country—and if there wasn't a reason, we'd find one. Many events were set outside among the vines, others on patios strung with café lights, and some soirées were in dimly lit wine cellars where we tasted straight from oak barrels. On every occasion there was plenty of food perfectly paired with the host's best wine du jour.

As you can imagine, vineyards and wineries were the most popular settings for—you guessed it—weddings. Weddings are considered the happiest of celebrations. And not only did we attend a lot of them, but we also hosted several romantic nuptial celebrations in our open-air, hilltop pavilion overlooking the vines. The most memorable of these special events was my niece's wedding in 2015. It was a big deal. The groom and his family, who were originally from France, were all in attendance, as well as many invited guests who had just flown in from Paris for the weekend-long festivities. Our east coast family and friends made the trek across the country as well as the west coast contingent of both the bride and groom who traveled up the coast.

A Wedding At Cana

We were expected to serve high-quality, wine-country fare and an abundance of fine wine to pair with each and every bite. And we did. What made it truly special was that we poured our very own *best* wine made from the hillside vines that the affair overlooked. The wine was a hit, and many people commented that they felt as if they were in the French Riviera. It was a weekend to remember.

On the third day there was a wedding at Cana in Galilee, and the mother of Jesus was there. Jesus also was invited to the wedding with his disciples. —John 2:1-2

During the first century, as it is today, weddings were considered the best of all celebrations. A wedding was a very sacred and joyous occasion; many lasted up to a week, and some even more. Weddings were a recognizable theme in the Bible and when Jesus told His "Parable of the Wedding" (Matthew 22:1-14), most people would have understood what He was trying to illustrate because he used a Jewish wedding as the setting of His story. The Wedding at Cana was yet another example of the importance of marriage celebrations.

Autumn was the ideal time for an ancient wedding feast because the harvest was in and the vintage finished, most of their work was done and they were ready to rest. Much like the weather we enjoyed in California, it was a season of cooler evenings making it comfortable to sit up late at night as we often did with a glass in hand and enjoying one another's company. More often than not the entire village came to a Jewish wedding. There was an abundance of food prepared, the wine flowed, and lots of music and dancing ensued.

I've always been curious as to why the first of all the miracles Jesus performed was turning water into wine at a wedding. The Bible chronicles many of the impressive miracles Jesus performed in His three short years of ministry. In John 5:19, Jesus declared that He couldn't do anything by Himself, but only through God the Father; this is when He walked on water, and it's attributed to His faith in God (Matthew 14:22-33). Another miraculous feat was feeding 5,000 people with five barley loaves and two fish. He healed the sick, made the blind to see, and raised the dead.

To some, it might seem insignificant that this feat of transformational magnitude was the first of His many miracles; taking a closer look, we begin to see that Jesus' ability to perform this miracle shows His real power. After all, this was the first sign of God's presence in the world through His Son, Jesus. And it is not a coincidence that wine is the elemental symbol of the blood of Christ— changing water into wine is a perfect prophetical scenario. Messianic prophecy is illustrated throughout Scripture right from the very beginning in Genesis.

A Wedding At Cana

> *When the wine ran out, the mother of Jesus said to him, "They have no wine." And Jesus said to her, "Woman, what does this have to do with me? My hour has not yet come." His mother said to the servants, "Do whatever he tells you."*
> —John 2:3-5

Jesus, His mother Mary, and the disciples were invited guests at a wedding in Cana of Galilee. The festivities would likely have started on the third day of the week and Jesus and His disciples apparently arrived a few days after it started. As the festivities progressed, the host family ran out of wine. This was a major faux pas of the times. As a wedding was supposed to be a joyous occasion and the best of celebrations, hospitality was extremely important, especially in providing good food and plenty of wine. Running out of wine presented a serious dilemma; it was a dishonor and a stigma that the family would have to live with for a long time.

Mary, who was probably a close relation to the bride, had come to Jesus and asked Him to do something to help the host; Jesus seems reluctant to do anything. Why? Some scholars say Mary long awaited the day when Jesus would miraculously demonstrate that He was the Messiah. Had she believed His "hour" had come? This statement infers that Mary no longer thought of Jesus merely as her son, but as the Messiah. Jesus knew that this one act of changing water into wine would ultimately reveal that

He was in fact *the* Messiah and would set off a chain of inevitable events that would change the world forever. Everything in Jesus' life was headed down the path for that final "hour" when He would be crucified.

> *Jesus said to the servants, "Fill the jars with water." And they filled them up to the brim. And he said to them, "Now draw some out and take it to the master of the feast." So they took it. When the master of the feast tasted the water now become wine, and did not know where it came from (though the servants who had drawn the water knew), the master of the feast called the bridegroom and said to him, "Everyone serves the good wine first, and when people have drunk freely, then the poor wine. But you have kept the [best] wine until now."*
>
> —John 2:7-10

The master of the wedding tasted what was given to him from the jars, and he was amazed when he realized it was the finest quality of wine.

Oftentimes at such events, the good, or high-quality wine is served first to impress guests, and once everyone is full and a little "tipsy," the cheaper wine is poured as no-one would likely notice. But Jesus produced a superior wine because of who He is; and it seems as if the groom gets credit for saving the best for last. But Jesus is the source of abundance as He appears as the true bridegroom at the wedding feast who served the best wine, providing abundance.

> *This, the first of his signs, Jesus did at Cana in Galilee, and manifested his glory. And his disciples believed in him.* —John 2:11

This miracle is not only my favorite because it revolves around fine wine, but because the wine He produced that day at the wedding of Cana points to His blood that was shed—it is God's presence in the world. From grafting and planting to harvesting and crushing into that final fermented wine, we experience the result of a tangible transformation, one that is presented to us at His table—The Lord's Supper. Much of what Jesus did through all His miracles was for the benefit of the disciples, so that they would believe. As we see in this first of many miracles, God's presence fills us "to the brim" as our lives overflow with His abundance. He *is* the Vine and the New Wine, a vintage that we will taste in heaven—the best of the best.

This is truly a foretaste of the feast to come.

> *On this mountain the Lord of hosts will make for all peoples a feast of rich food, a feast of well-aged wine, of rich food full of marrow, of aged wine well refined.* —Isaiah 25:6

What Would Jesus Pair?

Wedding food in first century Galilee was as important as it is today for us. When Rob and I were planning our wedding celebration, a relative said, "Don't worry so much about the food, no one will remember." But on the contrary they do. Food is a blessing far beyond sustenance, food unites us and feeds our soul.

While we do not know for certain what was served at that wedding at Cana in Galilee, the food of those ancient events would have been kosher and played an important part of their faith and culture. While most people seldom ate meat because it was a luxury, a wedding feast might have included roasted lamb and goat (which were otherwise reserved for festivals and sacrificial feasts like Passover). Game birds were prepared and depending where they lived, fish was on the menu; of course a variety of bread was offered alongside spiced lentil dishes. I can envision the plentiful Seven Species of the Holy Land being featured which comprised five fruits—figs, dates, grapes, pomegranates, and olives—and two grains, wheat and barley made into loaves.

And the wine? The wine was not only enjoyed by the newly married couple and their guests, but it was also used in sauces, breads, and various dishes to the delight of everyone at the wedding of Cana in Galilee.

The following suggested recipes spotlight the various food served at first-century weddings.

A Wedding At Cana

- Lots of Red Wine (Israeli wine from Galilee would be best)
- Seven Species Charcuterie
    - Solomon's Flatbread Crackers, page 255
    - Grape and Prosciutto Crostini, page 269
    - Olive Tapenade and Hummus, page 265
    - Goat Cheese Stuffed Dates, page 273
    - Brie en Croûte with Fig Jam (or fresh or 2 dried figs), page 271
    - Pomegranate Relish (with Brie or Manchego), page 274
- Lamb with Figs and Red Wine, page 314
- Creamy Pheasant with Fruited Israeli Couscous, page 310
- Mediterranean Spiced Game Hens, page 307
- Barley Cakes (biscuits), page 260
- Brown Butter Lentil and Sweet Potato Salad, page 288
- Song of Songs Nut Cakes, page 321
- Honey Almond Cake, page 317

11

Harvest of Plenty

You don't need to be a farmer to look forward to harvest. Growing up on the East Coast, autumn was a time of joy beginning with the state fair featuring the best produce of the Garden State. I have the fondest memories of my Aunt Evelyn who enjoyed taking us on adventures, especially apple picking in the fall. It brings back visions of bushels brimming with red, green, and even yellow apples just waiting to be enjoyed in as many ways as you can imagine. In school we sang harvest songs and made paper cornucopia to hang on the refrigerator. It was a crescendo of activity culminating with the long-anticipated Thanksgiving dinner—celebrating the autumnal harvest.

When we lived in Paso Robles, harvest was the most exciting time of the year. After all the flurry of constant work of the growing season, which essentially began after late winter pruning, we finally got to harvest our grapes. Everything that had been done in the vineyard led up to the most celebrated of seasons. The decisions made by the winemaker and the procedures in the winery were dependent on the outcome of harvest. Harvesting grapes to make wine was the last event in our vineyard, and the first step to becoming a finished bottle of wine—and it's also the busiest.

The first year we lived in Paso Robles, we wondered, "When *exactly* do you harvest wine grapes?" Everything was new to us that first year, including living on a ranch, surrounded by vines, on a dirt road, and encountering snakes, lizards, and tarantulas. When the tarantulas came out, and they did every year, harvest was around the corner. When do you really harvest wine grapes? It's not at the onset of tarantulas despite lore, but it depends on many other variables. Harvest began as early as August and continued through October, although one year we picked the last of our grapes in November. White wine grapes mature faster than red grapes making them the first grapes ripened, harvested, and sent to crush.

We measured sugar accumulation in the grapes on a daily basis with a refractometer (a small handheld device) to determine when the grapes were mature enough with the ideal level of sugar. This would have a profound effect on the final product. Sugar equals ripeness. Ripeness equals delicious wine.

The first day of harvest was always a big event and often started very early in the morning so that the sugars would remain steady. Crews came out in droves and worked steadily, hunched over with hand clippers cutting the beautiful clusters from the vine to fill the bins on the back of a tractor. There are two methods to harvest wine grapes, mechanical harvesting, and hand harvesting—we practiced the latter for quality control. It was hard work, but it was worth it.

Finally, when the picking was done it was time to party. The long weekend of our annual Harvest Festival was celebrated by all the wineries in one way or another with featured wine pairings, cellar tastings, special dinners, and music. It was always a remarkable time of year. Celebrating the harvest is a tradition that dates back thousands of years.

Ancient Harvest Festivals

The Bible is full of stories and metaphors about harvest, and the word itself is mentioned about sixty-nine times from beginning to end. Setting symbolism aside, the ancient people lived in an agrarian society and growing and reaping was at the center of their culture—it's what sustained them. A plentiful harvest was the reward for all of the hard work people had endured. Without a good harvest the effort that had gone into planting, pruning, and tending their crops, orchards, and vineyards would have been futile.

Harvesting was not a once and done event of the year as it was for us on the vineyard, the various crops and plants ripened at different times. In ancient Israel, it was entire families and communities who did the harvesting.

What Would Jesus Pair?

The Old Testament points to the various biblical laws as they relate to the ancient Israelites' seasonal crops and harvests. God's commands were very specific when it came to their crops. The major crops of the land that are listed in Deuteronomy 8:8 are wheat, barley, grapes, figs, pomegranates, olives, and (date) honey. These encompass the seven species of the Promised Land.

The spring harvest included herbs, legumes, and the most important crops of the season were the two cereal grains of the seven species, barley and wheat. These cereals were celebrated, but the newly harvested grains could not be eaten until the offering of the first fruits, and this occurred on the day after the Sabbath of the Festival of Unleavened Bread. *And the Lord spoke to Moses, saying, "Speak to the people of Israel and say to them, When you come into the land that I give you and reap its harvest, you shall bring the sheaf of the firstfruits of your harvest to the priest"* (Leviticus 23:9-10).

God had commanded the Israelites to celebrate a festival to Him three times each year.

First, in the spring they were to celebrate the Festival of Unleavened Bread. Next, they were to celebrate the Festival of Harvest with the first fruits of the crops from their fields. And finally, they were to celebrate the Festival of Ingathering at the end of the year, at harvest time. This was an ancient harvest festival.

> *You shall keep the Feast of Harvest, of the firstfruits of your labor, of what you sow in the field. You shall keep the Feast of Ingathering at the end of the year, when you gather in from the field the fruit of your labor.*
> —Exodus 23:16

Pentecost was also called the Feast of the Harvest and was celebrated near the end of the grain harvest, which included grain and loaf offerings. This is spelled out in Leviticus 23:16-17. The barley and wheat were planted in the autumn and ripened in spring, but barley matured faster and would be harvested sooner therefore making it the grain that was offered during the Festival of Unleavened Bread.

The summer harvest consisted mostly of the main fruits: grapes, olives, dates, figs, and pomegranates along with many others that were considered lesser. During the summer, they also gathered seeds and picked vegetables, but these were less common to the rocky, hillside terrain of the region that received seasonal rain. Scripture doesn't mention many gardens, cultivated vegetables, or even wild vegetable plants probably because of the lack of irrigation.

After the summer harvest, it was finally time for the autumn festivals; it was a celebratory time of great rejoicing. Autumn was set aside as a special time of celebrating not just the harvest, but this was the ideal time for a wedding—a time of great joy. The bulk of their work was done and the cooler evenings in the autumn months were preferable for celebrating. The wine grape harvest was complete, and wine was always associated with blessings and joy throughout Scripture.

> *You shall keep the Feast of Booths seven days, when you have gathered in the produce from your threshing floor and your winepress. You shall rejoice in your feast, you and your son and your daughter, your male servant and your female servant, the Levite, the sojourner, the fatherless, and the widow who are within your towns. For seven days you shall keep the feast to the Lord your God at the place that the Lord will choose, because the Lord your God will bless you in all your produce and in all the work of your hands, so that you will be altogether joyful.*
> —Deuteronomy 16:13-15

God created the heavens and the earth and the living things on earth; He created night and day, and He created the seasons. God is in control of the harvest time; it is part of His work, *"Let us fear the Lord our God, who gives the rain in its season, the autumn rain and the spring rain, and keeps for us the weeks appointed for the harvest"* (Jeremiah 5:24). God also used the lack of good harvest as the result of human disobedience.

Planting, sowing, growing, and reaping was at the center of life for our biblical ancestors as agriculture was basic to survival. They lived by the seasons. With the abundance of references to harvest in Scripture, we see an emphasis on symbolic meaning, and it points us to God's abundant provision. Jesus specifically refers to God as the Lord of the harvest. In doing so, He reflects the Bible's viewpoint on harvest when He entreats those who believe to ask God for laborers.

> *The harvest is plentiful, but the laborers are few; therefore pray earnestly to the Lord of the harvest to send out laborers into his harvest.* —Matthew 9:37-38

Jesus uses this harvest imagery to implore His followers to humbly pray, to ask God to call upon more workers, the faithful believers, to share the Gospel and bring home the spiritually lost. So, Jesus says, *"Pray earnestly to the Lord of the harvest to send out laborers into his harvest"* (Matthew 9:38). It's not surprising that the vineyard became a biblical symbol for the people of God. The most famous use of the vineyard symbolism in the Old Testament appears in Isaiah 5, where we are told, *"The vineyard of the Lord of hosts is the house of Israel."*

One year, when the boys were old enough, we gave them their own short row of vines to harvest. We had a "kid crew harvest party" and invited their friends to come pick grapes. We gave them gloves, shears, and big buckets to collect their fruit. They found out quickly just how hard it is to harvest grapes. Spencer and Alec always picked clusters of grapes and ate them right off the vine. Wine grapes are small with lots of seeds, but they are delicious when ripe.

We learned a lot about harvest in our years of living on a vineyard. There was a tremendous amount of work that went into the growing season, and there was something glorious about harvest. From the beginning, I understood the Scriptural context of harvest; if God is the Lord of the Harvest, then the land cannot produce fruit without abiding in Him. The vineyards are the mission fields, and we are the laborers. We produce fruit resulting from His grace and the work He does in us. God surely is the Lord of the Harvest. The quality of the harvest is only as good as our faith which produces good works.

The gathering of things planted at harvest time has since the beginning been a natural time of reaping not only that which has been sown, but also joy.

These suggested recipes celebrate the grains of harvest.

- Barley with Roasted Mediterranean Vegetables, page 292
- Egyptian Barley Salad with Pomegranate Vinaigrette, page 282
- Creamy Barley Breakfast Porridge, page 261
- Mediterranean Tabbouleh, page 284

12

I Am the Vine

I am the vine; you are the branches. Whoever abides in me and I in him, he it is that bears much fruit, for apart from me you can do nothing. —John 15:5

THE MORAVIAN GLASS WINDOWS ETCHED with the "I Am" statements of Jesus were a mystery to me as I sat and stared up at them in church as a child. Many churches of the era boasted stained glass windows or wooden panels of the Stations of the Cross, also known as the Way of the Cross. Some of these were impressive, a stunning display of art and a testament to the craftsmen who made them. The Stations are a series of images which depicts Jesus on the day of His crucifixion. The fourteen panels vividly tell the story of Christ's last day portraying the events in the Passion of Christ—beginning with His judgment by Pontius Pilate and ending as He is laid in the tomb.

The "I Am" windows, as I remember, were not brightly colored as so many were, and the hand-blown glass was both clear and frosted with bubbles; the images were embellished in a yellowish-golden hue, with black outlines and flourishes. In one particular window, vines elegantly wound throughout with a prominent cluster of grapes. The image was oddly interrupted by windowpanes, but it captured and held my imagination, nonetheless. What strikes me now is the impact that that specific, simple window reading only a few short words would have on my life one day—*I Am the Vine*.

While I always loved wine, and from early on my husband and I envisioned retiring on our own vineyard one day, it's one of those things that I really wondered could possibly come to fruition. Well, it did, and sooner rather than wait to retire. With a two-year-old little boy and another on the way, we were living the dream among the vines. Alec, our youngest, became known as our vineyard baby. In eighth grade, he chose as his life verse John 15:5, "*I am the vine; you are the branches. Whoever abides in me and I in him, he it is that bears much fruit, for apart from me you can do nothing.*"

When they were old enough, Alec and Spencer enjoyed their very own—very small—row of grapevines to watch bud, grow, and produce fruit as the respective seasons progressed. They learned to tend the vines, test the fruit sugar, and harvest grapes to make jelly (even though they had their own wine label—*Alec Spencer Cellars, College Fund*). It was a good lesson for them to experience the hard work and responsibility of caring for their vineyard and the importance of witnessing the rhythm of the seasons and the impact of nature on all living things.

One of the biggest thrills of living on a vineyard was walking through the long and perfect rows at different stages of growth. After pruning the bare branches to a mere inch at the end of winter, bud break was seemingly instantaneous, and the delicate tendrils would wrap themselves around the trellis wires for strength to bear the weight of the mature vine and forthcoming clusters of grapes. Witnessing this miraculous transformation in nature, I pondered the imagery of which Jesus spoke in His Word, "I Am the Vine." I could feel the presence of Jesus in the vineyard on many occasions. From the beginning, I wanted to know more about this simple "I Am" statement because I was part of it; I was the one of the branches He spoke of with tendrils reaching up to Him for support, and I knew He was the source underneath the soil—that which I couldn't see. I soon came to realize that I, like my vineyard, couldn't thrive or produce fruit without Jesus the Vine.

As it was with my childhood curiosity, I wanted to know more about why God would frequently use the image of a plant and vineyards. The vine has come to symbolize many things: determination, endurance, survival, progress, and blessings. In retrospect, I have been tested many times in life to the result of these attributes—Jesus the Vine provided all I needed to flourish. We see that flowers and vines are prominent Christian symbols which represent the blood of Christ, vineyards are the mission fields often mentioned in Scripture, and the grapes represent good works.

Grapevines are beautiful and prolific; they will grow and produce fruit for thirty to fifty years. A vine has a basic structure that includes roots, trunk, graft union, cordons, and spurs, but that is only scratching the surface of its intricate system. Grapevines are rarely (if ever) grown from seed since the desired grapevine genetics do not always carry over from the seed to the plant. Instead, grapevines are grown from rootstock cuttings.

The rootstock is the portion of the vine that extends into the soil and draws up water, nutrients, and minerals into the plant. For wine grapevines (Vitis vinifera), the vine, as a bud cut from a varietal (Cabernet, Chardonnay, Merlot, etc.) plant, is grafted onto the rootstock of another plant. A grapevine starts as two separate plants that are grafted together. This technique joins the tissues of two plants together so they continue to grow as one plant. Choice rootstock is essential to the vitality of the vine as it is chosen for properties which resist pests, extreme weather, and other detrimental conditions.

Grafting is a time-consuming process requiring patience and practice. Specialists cut a V-shaped slice into the flesh of the rootstock above the soil level. A tiny bud from the desired varietal plant is cut to match the slice in the rootstock. The bud is then placed in the notch and covered with tape to hold it in place with just the tip of the bud showing. The graft union grows together rather quickly—usually in a few weeks—and within a year, it is strong. The bud pushes and grows and once established, the rootstock above the graft union is cut away.

The two plants have now become one and can be planted in the soil. The graft union grows as the plant grows, but the healed scar from the process of grafting is always visible. Jesus said, *"I am the vine."* He is our rootstock, and we have been intentionally grafted into Him. The remaining scar on the base of the vine, on which each of us as a bud has been placed, reminds us of our own sanctification at the expense of Jesus. His energy flows through His wounds into our lives.

> *There shall come forth a shoot from the stump of Jesse,*
> *and a branch from his roots shall bear fruit.*
> —Isaiah 11:1

A healthy vine requires a healthy root system. Roots anchor a grapevine in the soil. The root system is delicate when first planted, but it doesn't take long before it is established, providing stability and nourishment. Smaller roots, or feeder roots, grow close to the surface while the large roots grow deep into the earth, down as far as fifteen feet, and spread horizontally. Grapevine roots are so strong that they can grow successfully in many kinds of soil and terrain, some even thrive on granite.

As the plant grows with the intricate root system, it begins to bear some fruit. You can't see the roots, as they're below the graft union—below the surface—but like the vine, the roots are always working, (even in the dormancy of winter). Jesus, our rootstock of the vine is always working in our lives, even though we cannot see His work.

In the Old Testament, vineyards represented the chosen people, Israel. They were time and again referred to as the vine that God brought out of Egypt and planted in the Promised Land (Deuteronomy 11:10). We see that the vine also represents Israel's fruitfulness—they were doing God's work on earth, and they were God's chosen people. Under His blessing, Israel, as the vine, developed deep roots, grew abundantly, and gave the relief of shade across the land. *"For the vineyard of the Lord of hosts is the house of Israel, and the men of Judah are his pleasant planting."* (Isaiah 5:7).

The Old Testament was prophetically fulfilled in the New Testament.

> *Israel was to flourish as a living example of how obedience bears the fruit of righteousness. By declaring Himself to be the True Vine, Jesus took the place of Israel, claiming to be the authentic, healthy vineyard the nation failed to become.* —Chuck Swindoll

Where Israel had failed, and failed they did, Jesus rose up as the True Vine in the Vineyards of the Lord to provide our salvation.

It has become abundantly clear that those vineyards of Central Coast California were God's mission fields where we were planted to live out our calling, even after we left. I would never have dreamed of the life I have now if God hadn't planted me in the hillside vineyards of Paso Robles; it was a new beginning, He had chosen me and was preparing me for my calling.

> *God said to Moses, "I am who I am." And he said, "Say this to the people of Israel: 'I am has sent me to you.'"*
> —Exodus 3:14

From the beginning, God has wanted His people to know Him. But if God wants us to know Him, why does He speak in metaphors—in figures of speech? The first time He calls Himself "I Am" is when He tells Moses who He is in Exodus. From then on, "I Am," as referenced to the identity of God, can be found over 300 times throughout Scripture. The seven "I Am" declarations of Jesus in the Gospel of John are powerful in their descriptions and help in our understanding of His identity.

In the last "I Am" statement, Jesus speaks of a vine. The imagery would have been recognizable to the people of Israel just as the wedding theme was in *The Parable of the*

What Would Jesus Pair?

Wedding Feast (Matthew 22:2), and His first miracle transforming water into wine at the Wedding at Cana (John 15). Vineyards are remarkable and abundant in many places on this earth, but especially in the Middle East. The cradle of wine civilization is the Fertile Crescent between the Tigris and Euphrates Rivers and even beyond. It reaches west to the Mediterranean Sea. The cultivation of grapevines in that part of the world is still important as it produces fruit, juice, and wine—wine being vital to the people of that land throughout history. This is where Jesus was born and lived His life.

It's intriguing how metaphors speak to our hearts in ways that disconnected events or circumstances cannot; it helps explain or infuse ideas with vivid descriptions through comparison and even symbolism. If I hadn't lived on a vineyard for ten years among the vines with a deeper intimacy with viticulture, my relationship with God would not be what it is today. "I am the vine" has revealed much more than my years living on a vineyard—the life of the Vine bears the truth of who we are in the sustaining power of Christ. As a bud is carefully grafted into the vine and planted in the right soil, being rooted in His Word brings life and fruitfulness.

> *I am the vine; you are the branches. Whoever abides in me and I in him, he it is that bears much fruit, for apart from me you can do nothing.* —John 15:5

These suggested recipes bring out the best of wine in cooking.
- Spiced Wine, page 263
- Wine Poached Pears, page 316
- Lamb with Figs and Red Wine, page 314

Section III

A CLOSER LOOK AT THE Promised Land reveals why it was sought after by God's chosen people, the Israelites, and the reason it is still considered a rich land of milk and honey today.

13

A LAND OF MILK AND HONEY

Then the Lord said, "I have surely seen the affliction of my people who are in Egypt and have heard their cry because of their taskmasters. I know their sufferings, and I have come down to deliver them out of the hand of the Egyptians and to bring them up out of that land to a good and broad land, a land flowing with milk and honey. —Exodus 3:7-8

EVERY TIME I MOVE, WHETHER to another state, town, or a new house, it's as if I can see promise on the horizon. While I've never left a place for a bad reason, there's always a great deal of excitement about the new one that I will soon call home. Each time, I'm invigorated by the idea of the new friends I will make, a fresh start, and a different community to explore. My leap from New Jersey to southern California in 2000 was a big one with tremendous cultural and culinary differences. Six years later, the 250-mile trek up the coast from Orange County to our vineyard in Paso Robles was not as drastic, but the vineyards and wine industry provided a fun new lifestyle.

What Would Jesus Pair?

Our biggest move from wine and cheese country to the corn and cows of Nebraska was a bit of culture shock, but we've loved our new home in the Midwest regardless.

The culinary culture in each location was notable with the food often reflecting the respective agricultural landscape. The east coast primarily celebrated the traditions of the immigrants who initially arrived through Ellis Island from abroad, especially Europe (Italy, Germany, Ireland, Poland...) In southern California we enjoyed a wide variety of ethnic food to include Mexican and Asian traditions, and seafood was frequently featured. Many dishes were prepared with tropical fruit and sauces, and the freshness of much of the cuisine seemed to mimic the weather—just right.

The wine country fare was fabulous and my favorite of all time. The food naturally paired with the wine of the region, especially when it was locally farmed. Eating in season and enjoying food and wine of the same viticultural area makes sense—they simply go together because of the terroir. Terroir is the characteristic taste and flavor imparted to a wine by the environment in which it is grown. I believe the same phenomenon holds true of all agricultural products. The local cheese was best when paired with local wine. Mission olives and olive oil, pomegranates, figs, and fruit from the central coast were especially tasty and perfect for pairing with other local food—but especially with wine.

A Land of Milk and Honey

Nebraska offers some of the best beef ever.

For the Lord your God is bringing you into a good land, a land of brooks of water, of fountains and springs, flowing out in the valleys and hills, a land of wheat and barley, of vines and fig trees and pomegranates, a land of olive trees and honey —Deuteronomy 8:7-8

The Promised Land is notably referred to as *a land flowing with milk and honey* in the Old Testament. This poetic language emphasizes the fertility of the soil, plenty of water, and the bountiful provision that awaited the Israelites—God's chosen people—after they had wandered the desert wilderness for forty years. The reference to milk suggests that there was ample pasture for the livestock to thrive; it symbolized nourishment and an agriculturally rich new life. Honey was frequently mentioned which infers that the bees had an abundance of pollinating plants to obtain nectar, the sweetness of a new life awaited them. It was a prosperous land of freedom and blessing, and the knowledge of the Lord was made clear to them.

The book of Deuteronomy specifically points out the Seven Species that were important in the Holy Land. Israel isn't just the land of milk and honey, but of wheat, barley, figs, dates, grapes, olives, and pomegranates, as well.

Shivat haminim is Hebrew for the Seven Species grown in the Holy Land, they are mentioned many times in the

What Would Jesus Pair?

Bible. For thousands of years, they have grown abundantly there. Today, these seven specific grains and fruits are crucial in the agricultural landscape and are customarily used in Israeli cuisine as well as religious celebrations and rituals still today. These seven species are special in many ways beyond their natural abundance in Israel, when eaten together, the seven species provide nearly all the nutrition a person needs to survive. I like to think of it as the ambrosia of the Holy Land—the nectar of God.

The human sense of taste encompasses receptors in the mouth that specifically pick up on five characteristics of taste: sweet, sour, salty, bitter, and savory. Scientific experiments have revealed that these five tastes indeed exist and are distinct from one another. The Seven Species together represent the entire range of these tastes. Preparing some of these foods together would create interesting flavor profiles, like a snack of sweet dates and marinated cured olives.

Many people like the taste of a chocolate covered pretzel that would be both sweet and salty, the same sensation sheds light on why salted caramel has become so popular. Asian cuisine has mastered this art, the combination of sweet and spicy in dishes or hot and sour in soups creates a delicious harmony. This is also how wine and food pairings work, you either mimic the flavor or juxtapose it. I discuss this further in the Art of Pairing chapter.

The Seven Species

The Seven Species that have played an important role in the food of the Israelites since they arrived in the Promised Land, the *land of milk and honey*, are all still abundantly available in the Middle East. Six of the seven species grow wild in Israel: wheat, barley, grapes, figs, olives, and dates. The origin of the pomegranate is not known, but as some Hebrew scholars have suggested, it might just have been the forbidden fruit in the Garden of Eden that Adam and Eve were tempted by after all. It's interesting to note that these particular grains and fruits ripen during the year in the order in which they appear in the Bible verse: first is wheat in the spring, and the last are olives and dates in the early autumn.

The Seven Species have taken center stage in religious traditions. Only their first fruits were acceptable offerings in the Temple. The following is a snippet of those very special seven—there is much more to these fruits and grains that deserves deeper exploration.

Wheat (*hitah*) and Barley (*se'orah*)

> *Now therefore the wheat and barley, oil and wine, of which my lord has spoken, let him send to his servants.*
> —2 Chronicles 2:15

Grains have always provided basic human sustenance—physically and spiritually. Wheat and barley are individually the foundational ingredients in bread which is the most important staple and universal food even in modern times—after all, bread is the staff of life. The cultivation of these grains can be traced back to the Holy Land. Most of the wheat grown around the world today comes from a type of wheat that is pretty much genetically identical to the species that originated in the Holy Land.

Bread plays a central role in Jewish and Christian rituals as we see in the Passover and the Lord's Supper. In both traditions bread is blessed before broken and eaten in the Seder or for communion. Barley was so important to our ancient ancestors that the harvest was celebrated on the second day of Passover. The Israelites would cut an *omer* (a measure) and bring it to the Temple as an offering. Bread's history and symbolism runs deep, and bread is a reminder that God is the provider of all. Bread was the staff of human existence. Manna was the Bread of Heaven that sustained the Israelites in the wilderness, and Jesus is the Bread of Life that sustains us this side of heaven.

Grapes (*gefen*)

> *And on the vine there were three branches. As soon as it budded, its blossoms shot forth, and the clusters ripened into grapes.* —Genesis 40:10

While grapes are not a necessity for survival unlike grain, this fruit of the vine does play a major role in the form of wine in the history and ritual of both Judaism and Christianity. Examples from the Bible start with Noah, in gratitude for being saved from the flood, he planted a vineyard; Abraham was blessed by Melchizedek with bread and wine; and the spies sent by Moses returned with a grape cluster so large that it required two men to carry it on a pole. The stories involving wine in Scripture seem endless. Like bread, wine is central to the Passover Seder and the Lord's Supper. It too is blessed before being presented. But my favorite story is the first miracle when Jesus turned water into wine at the wedding in Cana.

The grape harvest was a joyous time, and an abundance of wine and other food provisions was proof that the children of Israel had fulfilled the will of God.

Of the seven "I Am" statements of Jesus. In the Gospel of John, *"I Am the Bread of Life"* is the first, and *"I Am the Vine"* is the last. It is no coincidence that in the administration of the Lord's Supper, it is first His body that was broken and offered for us to eat and lastly His blood that was shed in the wine we drink, doing this in remembrance of our Savior.

Today the Holy Land shares the same vine-friendly climate as many other important wine-producing regions in the world including Israel, Greece, Italy, France, and our very own California.

Figs (*te'enah*)

> And they came to the Valley of Eshcol and cut down from there a branch with a single cluster of grapes, and they carried it on a pole between two of them; they also brought some pomegranates and figs.
> —Numbers 13:23

There is something rich and exotic about figs. The beautiful, deep hues, the distinctive shape and sweet, gentle smell are alluring. When we professionally photographed our *Sharp's Hill Vineyards* wines for advertising, we included luscious, ripened figs for a more appealing sense of quality.

Growing to nearly twenty feet in height and with large leaves, the fig tree provides pleasant shade. Mentioned over fifty times in Scripture, the fig tree was very important in ancient times as an agricultural product with high nutritional value. Making a debut in the beginning of Genesis, we see fig leaves in the Garden of Eden hiding the shame of Adam and Eve. Figs are the only tree specified that we know for sure was in the Garden.

> During Solomon's lifetime Judah and Israel, from Dan to Beersheba, lived in safety, everyone under their own vine and under their own fig tree. —1 Kings 4:25

The people from this large region (Judah and Israel, from Dan to Beersheba) were privileged to no longer live in barricaded cities in fear because of their enemies—they were spread out across the land, which they cultivated and were able to live off the fruits of their labor. Repeatedly in Scripture, we see the fig tree as a symbol of wellbeing and security; and along with the vine, its shade denotes the same sense of prosperity. No wonder it was featured among the Seven Species of the Promised Land.

Figs are a vitamin-and-mineral-rich fruit, considered one of the healthiest for the brain and body. Figs are a member of the mulberry family and in Israel, they ripen from June to the end of the year. The beauty of this fruit is that it is scrumptious when fresh but can also be dried. In ancient times, dried figs were often chopped and pressed into a cake. Israelites were known to have enjoyed fresh or dried figs every day. When I entertain, my favorite appetizer is fig jam spread over brie en croûte. When they are in season, fresh figs raise the quality of any dish, especially a charcuterie, to a level of elegance.

Dates (*tamar*)

This fruit is also called *dvash* (honey) in the Bible and mentioned fifty-five times.

> *In the course of time Cain brought to the Lord an offering of the fruit of the ground.* —Genesis 4:3

What Would Jesus Pair?

We had date palm trees in our yard in Southern California. At first it was really exciting and exotic for a Jersey girl, but unfortunately while they were tall and majestic, they were only ornamental. Date palms are common in the warm zones of the United States, and we had our share of them dotted along the West Coast—mostly planted for their aesthetic value. However, they are of major importance in the Mediterranean and Middle Eastern tropical regions as an agricultural resource.

Date palms enjoy a long life span up to 100 years and produce an abundance of fruit. It doesn't hurt that they are relatively resistant to pests and disease. They are considered one of the earliest plants that were cultivated by humans and provide more than just fruit, dating back 6,000 years, date palm wood was used to build houses, and the fronds were used as roof coverings on Middle Eastern houses.

Dates are eaten fresh or dried and contain many phytonutrients, vitamins and minerals, such as iron, potassium, A, K, and B vitamins, copper, magnesium, and manganese. A common sweetener known as date honey is made from boiling the dates for a long time to produce a thick, shelf-stable syrup that lasts a long time. The beauty of dates is that they are delightfully sweet, store well, and can be used in both savory dishes and desserts.

I have fond memories with my boys, tasting samples of all the varieties of dates from the local farmers market in

California. It became a ritual to bring home a bag of these gems rolled in coconut flakes as a sweet treat.

Olives (*zayit*)

> *Command the people of Israel to bring you pure oil from beaten olives for the lamp, that a light may be kept burning regularly.*   —Leviticus 24:2

While date palms were prominent in our southern Orange County home, Mission olive trees were plentiful on our vineyard property and throughout the community in Paso Robles. At first, they just produced a dirty ground covering for the birds to eat, but finally we learned how to brine those smooth, black olives and enjoy yet another culinary delight of wine country. Olive oil production in California has seen a renaissance since the 1990s (especially because of its health benefits), and as our wine region grew, harvesting and milling olives picked up pace. Olive oil production continues to soar, and olive oil tasting is an art which caught on fast with the culinary scene. At one event, I even tasted olive oil ice-cream—while not my favorite, it is interesting. Gifting one another olive oil has become a tradition with my family.

> *The olive tree is one of the plants most frequently mentioned in the Bible. Scripture writers used olive tree*

imagery to describe Jesus' Jewish roots and the relationship of Jews and Gentiles. When farmers cut down old olive trees (several hundred years old) to improve their future growth, new shoots grow from the old stump, and the tree begins producing olives again. This aspect of the olive tree provides an image of Isaiah's prophecy, "A shoot will come up from the stump of Jesse; from His roots a Branch will bear fruit" (Isaiah 11:1). As a descendant of David, Jesus was the shoot from the stump of Jesse (David's father).

—Ray Vander Laan
(thattheworldmayknow.com)

As the Old Testament frequently notes, the olive tree is beautiful (Jeremiah 11:16, Hosea 14:6). The faithful followers of God are compared to vigorous olive trees, and their children are said to be like the shoots that appear at the tree's roots, guaranteeing its survival. The New Testament uses olive trees to help illustrate God's plan of salvation. In Romans 11:11-24, Paul describes Christians as either natural olive branches (those of Jewish background), or olive branches that have been grafted onto Jesus (Gentiles). As branches grafted into Jesus, Christians will only bear fruit if we are attached to Him and have a personal relationship with Him.

Cured olives are not only delicious on their own and used in recipes, but they are also an important resource used as oil for sautéing and dressing foods, it is also used as an ointment for skin and hair—especially in ancient days—and it was the sacred oil used for lighting the eternal light above the ark where the Torah was kept. Many health-protecting nutrients have been identified in olives including antioxidant, anti-inflammatory and cancer-fighting benefits. Maybe that's why olive trees live hundreds of years?

Pomegranates (*rimon*)

> *Let us go out early to the vineyards and see whether the vines have budded, whether the grape blossoms have opened and the pomegranates are in bloom. There I will give you my love.* —Song of Solomon 7:12

Pomegranates grace our fruit bowl when they are in season. My boys love them. Some say they are the most beautiful of all the fruit in Israel—filled with ruby jewels. Pomegranates were often depicted in ancient mosaics, paintings, and architectural decoration. It's documented in Exodus that images of pomegranates were sewn into the High Priests robes, *"On its hem you shall make pomegranates of blue and purple and scarlet yarns, around its hem, with bells of gold between them, a golden bell and a pomegranate"* (Exodus 28:33).

In the Song of Songs, Solomon characterizes spring by the *"budding of the pomegranates,"* (6:11). Ancient coins in the first two centuries were minted with a single pomegranate, and today they are frequently used as a silver adornment on modern Torah scrolls as a remembrance of the Temple. Like olives, it was a suitable Temple offering because they ripen for harvest between Passover and Pentecost. As the top of a pomegranate resembles the shape of a crown, it's been associated with the Pentateuch—the first five books of the Torah written by Moses—which is considered the crown of the Torah.

In ancient Egypt the fruit was eaten fresh, and the juice was considered an aphrodisiac, additionally the sweet seeds fermented nicely into a delightful fruit wine. Pomegranate rinds were useful as a medicinal remedy for intestinal worms, and the flowers were used to produce red dye while the inner, yellow flesh was made into a stain for leather.

Today pomegranates are in abundance during the time of the fall feasts in Israel; a symbol of Rosh Hashanah (Jewish New Year) and the holiday season. They are ripe and ready, bursting to tell a story—a story that God wrote. Pomegranates have been held sacred in most of the world's major religions including Judaism, Christianity, Buddhism, and Islam. Rabbis have said that the fact that there is no flesh, only seeds, speaks of the blessings and commandments of God—they are not for our own selfish, fleshly desires, but for blessing others because once flesh is gone, it has gone forever, but when a seed dies, it produces a new life. A pomegranate reminds us that we are living for the benefit and blessing of others.

Today, pomegranates are mostly eaten fresh, often tossed into salads or as a colorful garnish, and often made into a juice or fruit wine. I like a tiny splash of pure pomegranate juice in a chilled glass of Prosecco (Italian sparkling wine). They are known for their medicinal properties including as an immune-system support and are rich in antioxidants and flavonoids.

The first Hebrews to settle in Israel after forty years of their wilderness wanderings were certainly onto something good with the Seven Species they found growing in their new land—the Promised Land—a land flowing with milk and honey.

> *Then the Lord said, "I have surely seen the affliction of my people who are in Egypt and have heard their cry because of their taskmasters. I know their sufferings, and I have come down to deliver them out of the hand of the Egyptians and to bring them up out of that land to a good and broad land, a land flowing with milk and honey.* —Exodus 3:7-8

WHAT WOULD JESUS PAIR?

Cooking with the Seven Species

> *Every day they continued to meet together in the temple courts. They broke bread in their homes and ate together with glad and sincere hearts* —Acts 2:46

Food is a symbol of hospitality, of God's provision, and a blessing to be shared with one another. The Seven Species exemplify God's abundant love in a magnificent way as we see when the Israelites arrived in the land of milk and honey, Canaan—The Promised Land.

These magnificent seven, as I like to call them, are versatile and the five fruits can be eaten fresh, stored and preserved for long periods. Figs, dates, and grapes can be dried, and the olives crushed, and when processed the olives make olive oil and grapes make a variety of wine. The grains, wheat and barley, are certainly not limited in range of either form or usage. They are all so special that they're considered valuable offerings in the Temple.

In researching recipes for these seven, I was overwhelmed by their versatility. While I have cooked with and served them all in one way or another, it was exciting to see what other people have created with them. As I experimented in the kitchen, I came up with my own versions of some of the ancient and unique recipes I found using mostly ingredients found in the Middle Eastern first century AD. I hope you will try them for yourself.

A Land of Milk and Honey

One thing that I enjoy offering at gatherings is a charcuterie, which is an appetizer assortment typically served on a wooden board or stone slab. It is usually eaten straight from the board itself. The board features a selection of preserved foods, especially cured meats or pâtés, as well as cheeses, fresh and dried fruits, olives, nuts, and crackers or bread. The history of charcuterie, as it pertains to cured meats, dates to the first century AD.

I have challenged myself to create a charcuterie using the seven grains and fruits according to the recipes provided. This closely resembles a mezze plate which is a Mediterranean version of a charcuterie. I've made bread from wheat and barley to use for crackers and flatbread. See if you can come up with your own version using all seven species.

WHEAT & BARLEY

There are six different classes of wheat: Hard Red Winter, Hard Red Spring, Soft Red Winter, Hard White, Soft White, and Durum. Each of these classes varies in its protein and gluten content. Wheat can also be used in other forms such as flaked and puffed for cereal, wheat bran, wheat germ, semolina for pasta, couscous, and bulgar. Try these recipes:

- Solomon's Flatbread Crackers *, page 255
- Mediterranean Tabbouleh Salad, page 284

GRAPES

A classic cluster of grapes makes any fruit and cheese board complete. What is a colorful fruit salad without juicy, plump grapes? Include them in a lightly dressed arugula salad with avocados and something special happens. But grapes are so much more when roasted and cooked. Enjoy these Greek-inspired dishes.

- Grape and Prosciutto Crostini *, page 269
- Dolmas—Stuffed Grape Leaves, page 267

FIGS

My mouth waters at the mention of figs. And there's more to the simple fig than meets the eye. Incorporate them into a salad or a variety of sweet and savory dishes and you have something out of the ordinary. Juicy, ripe figs are ideal for making homemade jams, preserves, compotes, and tangy chutneys. Fresh figs pair well with a wide variety of cheeses from soft to hard, from mild to bold—just pick your favorite and serve with a glass of wine—to make it an over-the-top experience, wrap halved, fresh figs in prosciutto. These exotic beauties will take center stage no matter how you use them, but especially when used in this way:

- Brie en Croûte with Fig Jam*, page 271
- Vanilla Fig Dressing, page 282

DATES

Dates had eluded me until I started using them. Chewy and sweet, dates are more versatile than I had realized—they can be added to cakes, puddings, compotes, and cookies, or used in stews, in grain dishes, or chopped into salads or breakfast cereal. I particularly like stuffing them for a holiday treat or an elegant appetizer. Date honey, a thick syrup to sweeten dishes including meats, is still used in Middle Eastern cuisine and comes in several forms. Try these:

- Goat Cheese Stuffed Dates*, page 273
- Song of Songs Nutcakes, page 321

OLIVES

Cured olives are a delicious snack and always served to guests in our home—I even have a special olive dish with a well in the center for the discarded pits. While I don't use olives in many dishes, tapenade is a favorite appetizer served alongside smooth and creamy hummus. A Greek salad is not a Greek salad without pitted black olives. Olive preservation is an ancient culinary tradition. You wouldn't want to eat an uncured olive because they are very bitter. Olives and olive oil are staple ingredients in the ancient and modern Mediterranean cuisine and today in wine country as olives and wine grapes require similar climates. Here's a few classic ways to use olives.

- Olive Tapenade*, page 265
- Classic Marinated Olives*, page 264

POMEGRANATES

Pomegranates are a most beautiful fruit enshrouded in mystery and human history. Although it's considered a one-of-a-kind delicacy, this fruit has many culinary uses beside eating the ruby, jewel-like seeds, called arils, fresh from the shell. Like citrus fruit, pomegranates taste very refreshing and can be bold in flavor and even a little tart which makes them ideal to toss onto salads, added to savory dishes, and even made into desserts. Pomegranate juice is loaded with nutrition as well as being delicious. A splash of pomegranate juice in a flute of champagne is simply delightful—or drop a few arils into the bottom of your champagne glass for an elegant treat.

Have you ever successfully eaten a pomegranate? It's not easy. My boys learned at an early age how to score, pull apart, and open a pomegranate in a bowl of water to make it less messy and much easier to get at the yummy seeds. Enjoy these fun recipes:

- Spiced Pear and Pomegranate Crostini*, page 270
- Chickpea Pomegranate Salad, page 290

* These recipes would be an ideal addition to a Seven Species charcuterie.

Section IV

Journey back through time to get a sense of what wine meant to the ancients, how it was made, and a glimpse of what it would be like to enjoy dinner with Jesus in the first century.

14

A GLANCE AT THE ANCIENT WORLD OF WINE

Let me sing for my beloved
my love song concerning his vineyard:
My beloved had a vineyard
on a very fertile hill.
He dug it and cleared it of stones,
and planted it with choice vines;
he built a watchtower in the midst of it,
and hewed out a wine vat in it.
—Isaiah 5:1-2

ROB AND I LOVE TO travel and have experienced many beautiful vineyards in our time together, but I would have cherished a visit to this vineyard of which Isaiah spoke. We have spent considerable time in Europe, and we've always sought out the local cuisine—and especially the wine of the region to pair with it. While not all countries boast the best wine, at least according to our palate, we have found the cuisine of most of these locales to be pleasurable. We especially look forward to trying new dishes for the first time, even when we can't pronounce them as they are written in their native language.

Having grown up drinking German wine, I thought I knew enough about it, at least until we visited and discovered the range of wine offerings of this country is more extensive than we had expected; we developed a new-found fondness for many German styles and varietals. The wine of France, well... it speaks for itself. The famous wine route in Alsace Lorraine was fascinating, and both the cuisine and wine are exemplified in a symbiotic intertwining of these two distinct cultures—both German and French. It was superb. While we have not spent as much time in the Mediterranean as we would have liked, we love the wine of Spain and Italy. Winemaking in these regions has been prolific for thousands of years.

Wine is as old as civilization and has had a major impact on shaping it from its origins in the Middle East and Mediterranean. Many countries in the Eastern Mediterranean continue to claim that they were first. Cyprus, Georgia, Lebanon, and others claim to be the cradle of wine, but the specific place of origin is really not important. What is significant is that wine had its origins in a part of the world and that it was readily accessible, giving way to its rapid spread to other nations.

We were invited by friends to Croatia in 2012, and subsequently fell in love with the landscape, the food, and the wine. While visiting their hillside vineyards, we were shown an ancient grapevine that survived the Phylloxera blight of the mid-nineteenth century which devastated most of Europe. It's as if this vine had a divine nature as it rose from destruction to life through the centuries, it was a holy vine indeed. According to one of the country's winemakers, Ivica Matošević, *"Like the country itself, Croatian cuisine has absorbed multiple influences, from the highlights of the Mediterranean diet to the hearty fare of Eastern Europe. Add to that the bounties of the Adriatic Sea, and you have one of the most remarkable arrays of gastronomic riches."* Likewise, the wine, being a diverse array of varietals and styles, each telling a story of their own, speaks of the multifaceted traditions and longstanding practices of this fascinating country.

Croatian wine has benefited from a long, 2,500-year history dating back to the ancient Greek settlers with their wine production on the southern Dalmatian islands. Like other old world wine producers, many traditional grape varieties still grow in Croatia, surprisingly mostly are white varietals and perfectly suited to the terroir. Our personal favorite varietals are Plavac Mali which is a red wine indigenous to Croatia, and Primitivo di Gioia which is the same red grape as our California prodigy, Zinfandel. The Greek writer Athenaeus wrote about the high-quality wine production of the Dalmatian islands some 1,800 years ago. They were certainly on to something special.

What Would Jesus Pair?

Viticulture in what is present-day Croatia existed around the time of the rise of the Roman Empire as it did in Central and Southern Europe. Some of the winemaking techniques we use today came from the Roman Empire and have influenced the craft globally. We see glimpses of the food and wine of the ancient Eastern Mediterranean cultures play out in our modern-day gastronomy. The Mediterranean diet has enjoyed a renaissance in the US and elsewhere around the globe, and not just for its health benefits, but for the epicurean aesthetic—it is simply beautiful food. Where there is quality food, there is quality wine to go with it.

A Holy Land of Plenty

> *It was a good land called Yaa*
> *Figs were in it, and grapes.*
> *It had more wine than water.*
> *Abundant was its honey, plentiful its oil.*
> —Story of Sinuhe

Isn't this a beautiful description of Yaa? Sinuhe, who wrote of this *good land,* was an Egyptian and a royal courtier who lived in the region and served the king and members of the royal family. He would have been intimately familiar with the Egyptian heritage of winemaking. The story is told in forty stanzas of poetic verse. This particular section is remarkable because Sinuhe was recounting the essence of life in the hill country of Syria-Palestine (the Holy Land) almost 2,000 years before Christ; it clearly emphasized that there was more wine than water in the place where His ancestors lived and traveled.

There is no doubt that from the beginning of time wine was an essential beverage and a major item of the early culture; this had to do with the fact that it was safer to drink than water. Cultivated grapes grew prolifically in the Mediterranean climate and conditions, and wine was considered a good gift of God. Evidence of this is found throughout the ancient world in archeological findings such as wine presses, wine cellars, wine vessels, and even grape byproducts. We know that the Eastern Mediterranean is considered the "cradle of wine," but there will likely always be some debate as to where exactly it started.

Many modern genetic scientists and archaeobotanists believe that the world's first known wine creation, that is turning grape juice into wine, is attributed to the people of the South Caucasus (Armenia, Azerbaijan, and Georgia). Other findings, however, credit the Greeks for the first winemaking endeavors as they domesticated wild grapevines about 4,000 years ago; it is likely that the Greeks developed a finer palate for wine resulting from their viniculture techniques. I would even say, the Egyptians shared the same verve for the art of making quality wine. Regardless of the various scientific methods and theories as to its true origins, identity of specific time and place of ancient grapevine cultivation, and the means of domestication, it is a foregone conclusion that wine was conceived in the Northeastern Mediterranean.

Archeological evidence is strong for wine production and consumption in Turkey as well, (the birthplace of the Apostle Paul), since the earliest of times. This would coincide with the theory that the first wine creation was in Georgia and Armenia which is just northeast of Turkey. The Hittites from Anatolia (modern-day Turkey) were first mentioned in the Bible in Genesis 23:10 (*Now Ephron was sitting among the Hittites, and Ephron the Hittite answered Abraham in the hearing of the Hittites, of all who went in at the gate of his city*), they were obviously known to the early Hebrews and especially Abraham. This culture shared an appreciation of wine and from their language comes what is likely the ancestral word for wine, *wiyana*, meaning grape and/or wine.

It's no coincidence that Abraham shared a legacy of vinicultural traditions with his sons and especially grandson, Joseph. He traveled extensively through prolific wine regions on his way to Canaan, and as we know was later blessed by Melchizedek with wine. From there the next generations were blessed by wine in one way or another.

When looking at the ancient world of wine, it's clear that Egypt has had a long love affair with this most sought out libation. Dating back thousands of years, wine played

A Glance At The Ancient World of Wine

an important role in ancient Egyptian ceremonial life. The wild grape (Vitis sylvestris) never grew in Egypt; however, a thriving royal winemaking industry was established in the Nile Delta following the introduction of grape cultivation from the Levant (ancient Canaan or modern-day Israel, Jordan, Lebanon, and Syria) to Egypt. The industry was attributed to the result of trade between Egypt and Canaan.

Egyptian hieroglyphics for grapes, vineyards, and winemaking, tell a story of a very sophisticated winemaking culture from its inception. Logograms, characters representing a word or phrase, were imprinted onto clay stoppers and what we would liken to modern-day wine labels. These *labels* which adorned the elongated wine jars or amphorae and left to ferment, were marked by volume and the amphorae themselves were decorated with rope. Some hieroglyphs depict what looks like winemaking paraphernalia such as the sack press. Other details of Egyptian winemaking and vinicultural practices are found in the paintings on the walls of tombs of the rich and famous. They depict the various stages of the trellised grapevines being tended, watered, and even picked in plump purple clusters.

Perhaps this, in addition to the jars of wine left in tombs, was another way to take their wine with them into the afterlife. And I thought you couldn't take it with you. It has been suggested that grapes were seen as a symbol of resurrection and may also have been thought to play a role in the transfiguration process of kings as part of their journey into the afterlife. Their beliefs of resurrection and transfiguration point to what happened to Jesus. Perhaps this was an unwitting Egyptian prophecy of our True King.

In ancient Egypt, it was mainly the upper classes and royal families who consumed wine. It was also used as an offering to the gods by pharaohs and priests. They believed it to have divine qualities. Moses would have been part of that class when rescued while floating in a basket on the Nile by Pharaoh's daughter. He lived in the Pharaoh's palace for the first forty years of his long life. He was taught about Yahweh, the God of Israel, as a child, but was raised to learn skills to one day become Pharaoh—wine would most definitely have been a daily drink. Looking further back in Scripture we see another Israelite, Joseph, while enslaved in Egypt, he interpreted the dreams of the royal cupbearer who was essentially an early sommelier. In this story we get a glimpse of one of the oldest forms of winemaking (Genesis 40:11). It's not surprising that Joseph became an ambassador of wine.

Early Viniculture and Viticulture

What's the difference? To clear things up, viticulture deals with the science of the cultivation, growing, and harvesting of grapes, while viniculture deals with this same science but specifically for wine production.

A Glance At The Ancient World of Wine

People began making wine early on in civilization by fermenting wild grapes. Alcoholic fermentation has been pursued by humans for thousands of years. Since ancient times, people have made the most of the natural fermentation process. It's interesting that fermentation occurs by itself in nature (without any help) in any sugar-containing fruit such as apples, berries, and... grapes. If left exposed in warm conditions, airborne yeasts act on the sugar to convert it into alcohol and carbon dioxide. This natural process was harnessed into a more controlled and deliberate pursuit.

While you can make wine from wild grapes, it isn't a generally practiced and will not achieve the quality of wine that we have come to enjoy. The main differences between wild grapevines (Vitis sylvestris) and domesticated grapevines (Vitis vinifera) are the size and sweetness of the grapes, pest and disease resistance (especially in modern times), and propagation. Wild grapes generally tend to have smaller fruit than domesticated grapes.

The domesticated grapevine, which is what we make wine from today, had taken hold in Syria-Palestine. From its inception—regardless of exactly where and when it occurred—viticulture spread to most of the Mediterranean and eventually the rest of modern-day Europe. This gave rise to the practice of viniculture—and the art of crafting wine was born. In ancient times it was a heavily traded product. The wine grape as we know it, is economically one of the most important cultivated fruit species in the world.

Wine was culturally important to our early ancestors who not only drank it as a main beverage, but used it in religious practices, for medicinal purposes, and incorporated the motif into art and sculpture. Furthermore, evidence of wine-drinking vessels has been found at ruins and burial sites. There is affirmation of ancient winemaking in the discovery of grape seeds, called pips, raisins, and additionally tartaric acid residue found in wine, and resins used to keep wine from spoiling because containers were not airtight. In these vessels, wine was stored and often underground for the cooler temperatures and moist conditions serving as a wine cellar of sorts. Some of those buried jars could remain underground for up to fifty years. This is reminiscent of the art of *laying down* a well-made wine in the cellar for many years and a testament to the innovation of those early winemakers.

Good Grapes, Good Wine

The horticultural skills of the early vintners were pretty remarkable as well. The wine industry saying holds true that, *"You can't make good wine from bad grapes, but you can make bad wine from good grapes."* In other words, good wine begins in the vineyard. The rocky hill-side terrain and limestone in which they grew their vines in the Syria-Palestine region and beyond was ideal along with the rainy seasons and months of sunshine. Our vineyards were grown in nearly the same conditions as Central Coast California wine country in the rolling hills of rocky limestone soil, with a short rainy season called el niño, and months of sunshine. The hot days and cool evenings provided the perfect conditions for flavorful, fruit forward wines. I do believe Jesus would have liked our wine.

Under the Roman Empire, wine production grew, and winemaking techniques were perfected, making it increasingly important as it was exported to other parts of the empire. This was early wine branding at its finest harkening back to the Egyptians.

It was the Greeks and Romans who ultimately spread wine throughout the Mediterranean and the significance of it continued to grow along with production. Wine became an important item of trade around the entire ancient world. It was, however, the Romans who firmly rooted the prominence of wine throughout this part of the world after they defeated the Greek empire. By 125 BC, the Romans occupied or had control of the entire Mediterranean basin. We see this domination by the Romans play out in the life of Jesus and His disciples.

The Romans believed that wine was a daily necessity and eventually this opinion prevailed throughout the empire; in its various forms, this *beverage of choice* was available to all people of all classes including slaves, peasants, and aristocrats. Men, women, and children alike drank wine. Romans and Jews respectively drank wine. The quality of the wine one drank differed however, based on class and status. To ensure the steady supply of wine to Roman soldiers and colonists, viniculture and wine production rapidly spread to every part of the empire. The Roman imperial system created an international market, and wine was a main commodity, it had become a brand in itself. This is what set the backdrop for the wine of the first century, and especially in the wine Jesus would have experienced throughout His travels. As He ate meals and drank wine with all classes of people, He experienced a variety of styles and caliber of wines.

The Manner of God(s)

While the Jews were monotheistic worshiping only Yahweh, the God of the Israelites, the Romans had a plethora of gods. The religion of Rome was vastly polytheistic, with all manner of gods, lesser deities, and guardian spirits influencing almost every aspect of life—including the consumption of wine and the vineyards. Interestingly, Dionysus, who was the Greek god of fertility, later became known as the god of wine (and pleasure). The Romans called him Bacchus. Bacchus journeyed far and wide. Everywhere he went he planted vines and taught the people viniculture—winemaking being the main motivation.

The ancient Greeks and Romans considered wine to be *golden nectar*, the drink of the gods, which symbolized immortality and victory over death. It is thought by some scholars that by 139 BC the Jews in Rome outwardly worshiped God, Yahweh, as Bacchus, as a means to detract from their Roman neighbors becoming suspicious of Judaism. I personally have a hard time coming to terms with this as the Jews were profoundly convicted in their faith. But, if this is in fact true, it's an interesting foreshadowing of a god, Bacchus, offering a means of everlasting life, propitiously pointing to Jesus when He raised a chalice of wine symbolizing His blood for the forgiveness of sins. The very next day, Jesus' blood was shed, and the third day, He rose, giving us victory over death.

The beginning of the biblical wine trail is Genesis. It unfolds in a garden, lush with fruit—and God saw that it was good. In researching the origins of wine, I have discovered a dramatic and fascinating story which unfolds over thousands of years. The life of Jesus exemplifies wine's centrality in the human story. From Noah planting the first vineyard, to Moses, Abraham, Joseph, and Jesus, we see a long tradition that transformed the Holy Land and its inhabitants. Wine is a dearly celebrated and essential part of life. We not only see its role in the vineyard, the rites and rituals of the church, and the joy of celebrations, but in its divine purpose.

The long history of viniculture shines light where the vine itself is sacred.

What Would Jesus Pair?

In Vino Veritas
In wine there is truth

15

DINNER WITH JESUS

Eating a meal together can be a place of joy, celebration, and friendship—we can show love for each other and celebrate life. —Jean Vanier

DESPITE MY FONDNESS FOR THE gastronomical experience of planning, preparing, and pairing meals, I do love a good potluck. This is something that I had always associated with boring suppers in the dank church basement that often left much to be desired. Just how many potato dishes, green bean casseroles, and Jello salads (an anomaly for sure) can anyone really wash down at one meal with watered-down lemonade? But I must admit, the potluck of the past has seen a renaissance of late. I recently discovered a fun potluck website called *Perfect Potluck* and it boasts not only great ideas and recipes, but also a sign up so you don't end up with five versions of macaroni salad, four corn dishes, an assortment of cookies, and no protein. For a gal who is carb-conscious, this is a dilemma I have experienced more than I care to recount.

What Would Jesus Pair?

In the generation and culture from which I hailed, the host or hostess provided the meal from soup to nuts. My mother hosted all the family holidays and was always really good at it, even her timing was impeccable, everything came out to the table at the same time, and it was perfectly plated and warm. I became very good at it too, especially planning the perfect combination of flavors, colors, and aromas. It took me a long time to actually say "yes" to invited guests when they offered to bring a dish. I almost felt guilty. Admittedly, I was won over, especially in wine country where most of our friends brought wine-friendly food. Now I am prepared with an answer when someone asks what they can bring—salad, side, or dessert. Regardless of what I take to someone's home, I always include a bottle of wine.

Fortunately, the potluck of today is nothing like that of the past—it has benefitted from a culinary facelift thanks to the likes of Pinterest and a desire for beautiful, quality food to share with our friends. Food is good for the soul. I love to get together and enjoy new and often exciting dishes and I especially appreciate the creativity of others. The best part is walking away with recipes to add to my repertoire that I might not have stumbled upon myself. Food truly does unite people in ways that nothing else does—and not just around the table, but side by side in the kitchen, chopping, mixing, sautéing, and tasting.

DINNER WITH JESUS

"Food... It has a culture. It has a history. It has a story. It has relationships."   —Winona LaDuke

The culinary history of the first-century Middle East is important because it shows us who we are in light of the Rabbi named Jesus whose culture influenced many of our traditions today, whether we know it or not. If we could travel back in time and share a meal with Jesus in His hometown in Galilee, what would be on the menu? Would Jesus cook it Himself or would it be a communal meal more like a potluck we have come to enjoy today? I wonder if the disciples had a penchant for cooking... What was their specialty, and what kind of wine would accompany this ancient Epicurean experience? Could you imagine sitting down to a meal with Jesus Himself blessing the food and the people sharing it.

Oh, how I wish I had a time machine, but as I don't, my speculation will have to do. I am sure Peter and Andrew would have provided the fish, Matthew would be in the background, and John would be right next to Jesus, *the one He loved most*. There is a lot we do know about the food and customs of the people of the ancient Mediterranean basin. We know that the food was kosher for the Jews, according to God's law, and dietary staples were legumes, fruits and vegetables, dairy products, fish, and game and meat when available. One thing that was most definitely served at every meal was bread, wine, and olive oil—the Holy Trinity of food.

A Look at the Laws of Leviticus

The Mosaic dietary code was important to the first-century Jews because God had handed down the law nearly fourteen centuries prior as it was according to His will and represented healthy guidelines; it revealed God's care for the physical and spiritual health of His people. Today our understanding of the medical reasons behind God's laws regarding animals or combinations of foods is limited, although some are pretty obvious—bats, monkeys, camels, and rats each come with potentially catastrophic consequences such as Ebola and other viruses among other serious maladies.

We have come to discover that the scientific wisdom behind this code has been seldom taught or explained. In Exodus, however, we learn that God chose the nation of Israel and set them apart for His special purpose (Exodus 19:5-6), and the dietary laws are attributed to His divine purpose: *"I am the Lord your God, who has separated you from the peoples. You shall therefore distinguish between clean beasts and unclean..."*

So, if you were having a meal Jesus and the disciples, pork, among other animal proteins, would not be on the menu.

One thing to keep in mind is that Jewish children were taught the Torah starting at age six, and by the time they were ten, would have been expected to have memorized most if not all of the first five books written by Moses: Genesis, Exodus, Leviticus, Numbers, and Deuteronomy. This is known as the Pentateuch.

> *And the Lord spoke to Moses and Aaron, saying to them, "Speak to the people of Israel, saying, These are the living things that you may eat among all the animals that are on the earth."* —Leviticus 11:1-2

The book of Leviticus was the first of the books studied by a Jewish child, and as such would have been studied by Jesus. The overall message of this book is sanctification—having been made holy by God. Moses communicates that receiving God's forgiveness and acceptance should be followed by holy living and spiritual growth. Now that Israel had been redeemed by God, they were to be purified into a people worthy of their God. *"You shall be holy, for I the Lord your God am holy,"* says Leviticus 19:2.

Leviticus explains how holy people should worship and what they could eat, and that included offering sacrifices which was a main activity of the temple. Only priests could offer sacrifices, but the sacrifices were provided by worshipers. They brought them (animals, wine, grain, oil, etc.) to an appointed place at the temple and handed them over to the priests, who in turn made the sacrifice. Jesus would have witnessed this practice as a child when He was in Jerusalem.

Each of the five offerings served as God's gracious provision for how one could regain and sustain fellowship with God. They include:

- Burnt offering
- Grain offering
- Peace offering
- Purification offering
- Guilt offering

If an Israelite wanted to give God thanks for being good to them and giving them life, they would have to offer something called a *free will sacrifice*, that is spilling the blood of an animal. It is reminiscent of God commanding Abraham to sacrifice his only son whom he fathered at the age 100. God in His mercy however, spared Isaac because of Abraham's obedience. This sacrificial practice is also what we see nearly 1,800 years later when Jesus was celebrating the Passover in Jerusalem. The sacrificed lamb was roasted and eaten according to strict guidelines. But the offerings in Leviticus had their ultimate fulfillment in Jesus when He sacrificed Himself, spilling His own blood. Hebrews 10:10 tells us this, *"And by that will we have been* sanctified through the offering of the body of Jesus Christ once for all."

After that, the temple was destroyed in AD 70 for a second and final time. No sacrifices have been made there since, because there is no longer a temple—lambs are no longer offered up.

The specific dietary laws that God handed down through Moses to communicate to the Israelites were detailed and spelled out in Leviticus 11:1-17. I will spare you the details, but they included specifications regarding animals, fish, birds, and insects—what they could and, specifically, what they could not eat. Believe it or not locusts were considered kosher according to this Mosaic law, and Jesus' cousin, John the Baptist, lived on locusts and honey. Jesus would have obeyed these laws considered to be kosher, and they did not only give guidance to the specific kind of food itself, but how it should be prepared.

The Company Jesus Kept

> *And as Jesus reclined at table in the house, behold, many tax collectors and sinners came and were reclining with Jesus and his disciples. And when the Pharisees saw this, they said to his disciples, "Why does your teacher eat with tax collectors and sinners?"* —Matthew 9:10-11

What Would Jesus Pair?

It is not ironic that it was Matthew who would be writing about Jesus eating among tax collectors and sinners. Matthew had been a despised tax collector when Jesus called him to follow Him (Matthew 9:9), and he proceeds to write about it in his own Gospel message. The very next verses describe Jesus reclining with tax collectors and sinners—this occurred in the home of Matthew when he invited Jesus and his fellow tax collectors among other *sinners* to dine with them. Matthew was known to be self-effacing, however he is not pointing out his own sinful nature here, instead he highlights the mercy Jesus showed by exalting the humble and laying low the proud. Jesus saw something in Matthew that no one else had—Jesus saw something in all of the disciples. Jesus sees something of true worth in all of us.

Jesus shared meals with many people throughout His life, but a closer look at those He *broke bread with* in the three years of His ministry reveals a vast spectrum from the rich to the poor, the pious to the humble, and the righteous to the sinner. I believe that part of this has to do with the fact that sharing a meal with others creates a bond. At the dinner table, everyone is equal. It is a time for conversation which in turn opens up the opportunity to forge community. The meal truly unites.

Jesus used food, farms, vineyards, and wine as a theme or setting in many of His Parables. Interestingly, it was Matthew who shed light on these Parables. We learn of the problem with keeping new wine in old wineskins (9:16-17); and, in Chapter 13, we learn of the weeds among the wheat and the kingdom of heaven being like a mustard seed, of leavening or yeast, and a net catching fish. Matthew 20 goes on to highlight laborers in the vineyards, and Chapter 21 describes a landowner who planted vineyards. Jesus even uses a celebratory marriage feast in one story, and a budding fig tree in another. Many of these Parables of Jesus are also told by Mark and Luke—with a crescendo telling of the prodigal son returning home and his father throwing a huge feast celebrating his return (Luke 15:11-22).

As much as I have come to appreciate a potluck for the variety of food and fellowship, our twenty-first-century, American fare is no match for that of a first-century communal spread. Imagine getting together with friends dining alfresco, relaxing at a table set with a charcuterie of Eastern Mediterranean olives, bread, cheese, fruits, nuts, and spreads, not to mention the aroma of exotic spices filling your senses, and of course wine from Israel, Turkey, Lebanon, or Greece.

Just thinking of this transports me to a distant time over 2,000 years ago when Jesus would have been reclining around a table with friends and strangers as they passed around platters of food and engaged in lively conversation. Just close your eyes and ponder what it would be like sitting next to Jesus, dipping the warm flatbread He

What Would Jesus Pair?

just broke and handed to you in a dish of oils and spices. How would you respond if He poured you a cup of wine? Breaking bread and sharing a meal establishes sacred bonds. Sharing a meal with Jesus is where worship happens—it's where life happens.

Scripture gives us a glimpse of what the first-century culinary scene was like. The Hebrew diet was mostly vegetarian, not so much for health benefits, but for economical purposes. Meat was reserved for special occasions. Most households had few animals, as they would have been heavily relied upon for milk, and their hair or wool; some were set aside for sacrifice offerings. Wild game would have been an alternative to their domestic stock animals. Fish was an important addition to their diet, as was the byproduct of the fish as they would have made fermented sauces and used the bones for various purposes.

The Seven Species found in Deuteronomy would have been plentiful and used with frequency when in season. As previously mentioned, olives were likely cured, and olive oil used for culinary as well as non-culinary purposes such as lamp oil, medicinal salves, and temple offerings. Grapes were eaten fresh, dried into raisins, and the juice fermented into wine. Wheat and barley were predominant grains and either ground into flour or added to dishes. They also cultivated spelt and millet; we still look to ancient grains for their nutritional value. Dates, figs, and pomegranates were eaten fresh, dried, and made into spreads, sauces, cakes, and even honey.

The first-century Mediterranean diet was not bland. There was an abundance and variety of fruits, vegetables, grains, legumes, nuts, and, even though not as prevalent on a daily basis, proteins to satisfy a healthy diet. Milk and milk products like butter, cheese, and yogurt were part of the daily diet and often eaten for breakfast. Seasoning food and wine with spices was not uncommon, and wild and cultivated herbs added even more dimension to their culinary practices as did the use of vinegar. Salt was the primary seasoning as it is today. And yes, they liked sweets. While they did not have a sweet tooth to meet today's standards, they enjoyed foods sweetened with honey, fruit syrups and juices, and dates and figs made delicious slurries and cakes.

While it seems as if they had a variety of ingredients available, much depended upon locale and wealth. Some spices were more exotic or harder to come by, so it was the wealthier in society who had access. They mostly prepared basic daily meals based on what was readily available. They essentially had to eat what was in season, unless it was dried, cured, or made into a honey, sauce or condiment such as vinegar. Their utensils were simple. Meals were prepared in open courtyards equipped with simple earthen ovens to bake their breads. Some communities shared courtyards for baking. Oftentimes breads were

What Would Jesus Pair?

baked on hot stones, which were also used to boil or stew their foods—a favored method. They did some roasting and frying, but this was reserved for special meals. Women did most of the cooking in the households. Jesus and His disciples prepared many meals, and they cooked while on the road when they were not invited guests.

I can't help but mention that in *The Chosen* series, meals and zealous preparation seem to be very prevalent.

So, what did Jesus actually eat at the Wedding at Cana, at Matthew's house, or while traveling with His disciples? Roasted lamb was featured at Passover and bread and wine was plentiful for sure, but many details elude us. There are numerous books, articles, and mostly speculation about the food served at these events, but what we do know is that the first-century Eastern Mediterranean was a land of abundant food. We know that Jesus and His disciples ate many meals together and I would speculate there was a lot of teaching during those precious moments. Jesus fed 5,000 people with five loaves and two fish. He made a breakfast of fish for His twelve as He waited on the shore, He attended celebrations and religious feasts, He ate with the Pharisees, with Mary, Martha, and Lazarus. He ate with sinners. Jesus even fasted.

Many books, movies, and sermon series have been written about dinner with Jesus which are all beautiful allegories of Jesus' invitation to follow Him. When He invited the disciples to join Him, He said to each of them,

Dinner with Jesus

"Follow me." And when they did, they spent much time walking and talking and sharing meals with their teacher.

I discovered how we can all have dinner with Jesus—not that everyone will jump at the invitation—but I will most definitely be among the first to RSVP.

> *To "have dinner with Jesus," is more of a metaphor of the joys and delights of being with Him in His kingdom, dining at the Messianic banquet that He provides throughout all eternity. The Book of Revelation refers to it as the marriage supper of the Lamb (Rev. 19:9) and makes it clear that you will want to be there. Jesus Himself referred to it in Luke 13:28-29, where He said that people from all corners of the earth will dine with Abraham, Isaac, and Jacob in the kingdom... I want to show you how you can be sure that there will be a place at the table with your name on it.*
>
> —Steven J. Cole (bible.org)

While I would give anything to host a dinner for Jesus and the disciples at my home with my family around my table, I know that won't happen this side of heaven—lest I be *entertaining angels unaware*. But someday, along with all who believe, I will dine at the eternal table of His kingdom. In the meantime, I will simply use my imagination and continue to wonder, What Would Jesus Eat?

16

WHAT WOULD JESUS DRINK?

Wine makes every meal an occasion, every table more elegant, every day more civilized. —Andre Simon

I TRULY BELIEVE WINE IS a good gift from God and that, while living on earth, His own Son Jesus enjoyed it.

"What did it taste like?" God did *bring forth wine to gladden a man's heart*, so it must have tasted pretty good. Taste matters. My husband and I, while having made the same wine from the same vineyards, have very different palates for wine. I am a wine snob and well, he's not. Needless to say, I was the one who designed the various blends for our winery alongside our winemaker. I penned this quote many years ago for a Wine Enthusiast contest: "*What is Wine? Wine is an art that begins in the vineyard and ends with your experience.*" Rob and I experience wine similarly in many ways, but truly hold a different opinion of the style or quality of what we like in the glass.

While I've tasted a lot of wine in my lifetime, there are some that I have never had the pleasure of experiencing. It's hard to believe that there are over 10,000 different varieties of wine grapes in the world today. Every one of those grape varieties is unique to the region where they are grown and the hybrids that are produced by grafting. *Pinotage* is a delicious wine that comes to mind, it is a red wine grape that is South Africa's signature variety and was cultivated there in 1925 as a cross between Pinot Noir and Cinsaut. The grapes used to produce certain wines are characteristic of those respective countries. The wine from Portugal is very different from the wine from Austria and the wine from Germany is very different from the wine from Spain—yet they are all considered Old World wines.

When studying for the sommelier blind tasting tests, I was trained to tell the difference; I could immediately tell the difference between Old World and New World wines—it's not as difficult as it sounds. New World wines are those produced outside of the traditional wine-growing regions of Europe and the Middle East, they are mainly Argentina, Australia, Canada, Chile, Mexico, New Zealand, South Africa, and the United States (primarily California). New World wines are usually fuller-bodied, higher in alcohol, have lower acidity, and show much riper fruit on the palate.

Old World wines tend to be lighter-bodied, lower in alcohol, have brighter acidity, and show more earth-driven flavors. Old World wine by today's standards, does not mean ancient—although ancient wine hails from the Eastern Mediterranean. So, what's the difference between today's Old World wine and ancient wine? There is a huge chasm between the two.

Lynnsay Maynard relates a fun story from inside the Boston Wine School in a class on Ancient Wine taught by Jonathon Alsop.

> He opens a red blend from Lebanon. *"This is something that citizens in biblical times would not have been acquainted with—the screw cap,"* he jokes. As Alsop opens a bottle of Italian wine, he explains to his students that the wine they are sampling bears little, if any, resemblance to wine during Christ's time. *"It's clean. It's clear. It's in a bottle,"* says Alsop, holding up the wine glass and examining it. *"These [ancient] wines were shipped around the Mediterranean in ceramic or wood casks; they would have taken on that flavor."*

The wine Jesus drank was not fined and filtered and was poured from a wineskin or earthenware vessel on most occasions. It didn't taste like the wines, even from what we consider *Old World*, we have come to appreciate today. We know that wines were being made in the Holy Land region and that included Galilee where Jesus and the disciples spent most of their time together. Details of the winemaking process of the Holy Land are debated by the experts though. The winemaking process had a big effect on the final product as did the type of wine. As Jesus traveled, He would have experienced a variety of wine depending upon the region.

The art of winemaking, carried out by all cultures including the Israelites of the first-century Roman Empire, influenced the entire Eastern Mediterranean. It was the culmination of the many centuries and societies of viniculture leading up to it. Archeological evidence shows that wine was produced throughout ancient Israel as part of the empire. The Jews most definitely made wine. While the specific onset of domestic viticulture in the empire is not clear to historians, it is likely that the Greeks had major influences through early settlements in southern Italy dating around 800 BC. In fact, this may have been why Greek wine was so important in ancient Rome. Though plenty of wine was made in Italy, it sold for a much lower price than what was made in Greece (before they were defeated by the Romans).

The ancient Greeks and Romans considered the consumption of wine as a staple of everyday life and respectively encouraged their colonies to plant vineyards for local use and trade. At the height of the Roman empire's production of wine, it's estimated that 47 million gallons of wine were consumed each year. That equates to nearly a bottle of wine every day for each person. That's a lot of wine.

As Italy grew a considerable number of indigenous vines, they embraced the ideal opportunity for wine production. The Greek name for the prolific southern region was Oenotria meaning "land of vines." Today, Italy still boasts the most varieties of wine grapes in the world—ten times more than France. As the Romans made allies of their conquests as a strategy to maintain strength and allegiance, their winemaking was influenced by the viticultural skills and techniques of those various cultures making it even more effective.

Just as modern culture experiences a variety of wine styles and quality, some mass produced, some hand-crafted, and a lot in-between, so did the ancients. The Roman wine industry would have had a huge influence throughout the Mediterranean basin as it was mass produced and shipped all over by the time of Christ—they cornered the market. Also, much of it was made by pretty high standards because of the wealth of the empire producing it. For instance, their sophisticated methods of using barrels and viticultural techniques allowed them to make more for less cost. The ancient city of Pompeii was one of the most prolific winemaking centers of the Roman world. It was a wealthy city, and they fervently worshiped their god of wine—Bacchus. Jesus would have had His share of Roman-influenced wine.

Making Wine

In order to know what the wine that Jesus drank tasted like, it's important to know how that wine was made. For me, there was nothing more exciting than being at the winery during harvest when the grapes were delivered to the crush pad. Half-ton bins, brimming with plump and beautifully shaped clusters, whether red or white, make my heart skip a beat. To taste a wine grape at the peak of ripeness is second to none. It's sweet, but not too sweet; it's balanced with layers of flavors that make it perfect for wine. Grapes are destined to become wine.

Winemaking, as it is today, took place in the autumn as the grapes would have ripened around September. White grapes are usually picked first, often in August, as they ripen faster than red. Immediately after they are harvested, grapes are crushed. Crushing is the first step to turning grapes into wine and this is when you break the grapes so the juice, pulp, and seeds can mingle with the skins of the grapes, the byproduct is called must. Ideally, the crush occurs immediately as temperature, conditions, and exposure to oxygen affect the wine even at this early stage. Pressing is the next step in the process that separates the grape juice from the fiber and other grape solids (or the must). In ancient winemaking the juices would have flowed into a wading pool where it was scooped out and placed in beeswax lined clay pots sometimes packed with honey and spices.

What Would Jesus Drink?

In winemaking, then and now, there are many variables that affect the process, and this includes the equipment used. Ancient wineries would have crushed and pressed their grapes in relatively similar ways as we do today, and some of their methods are the forerunner of today's techniques. Beside the available grape varieties, the financial resources would play into many of the decisions of how to best carry out the craft. When our winery was in full swing, we preferred using techniques and tools that would help us make really great wine according to our budget and size. With that said, because we were a boutique (small and handcrafted) winery, our resources were taken into consideration when making decisions like using high quality oak and the longevity in the barrel before bottling to name a few. In some ways we had a great advantage.

The romantic vision of stomping on grapes to crush them was a reality for the Romans. While tools like the sack press were used earlier by the Egyptians, the Romans would have mostly used a vertical basket press (think of it as a huge apple press) in the next phase. Many of our modern stainless-steel presses are based on these ancient wooden models. The southern colonies of Greece probably brought their own wine pressing methods with them which influenced the Roman Empire. The crushing and pressing technique would have influenced the final product. When we made our rosé wine, we used a method to get "free run" juice, which definitely yields a somewhat softer mouthfeel for our French-style wine—the ancients also used free run juice for some of their better wines. When you press the grapes increasingly harder, different compounds are extracted including tannins and phenolics, compounds which affect the color, feel, and taste of the wine.

The juice that ran from the press was called mustum (vinum), meaning "new (wine)," it was often drunk unfermented, as sweet cider is by today's standards. But when it was reserved for wine, it was placed in the enormous (105 gallon) clay pots or vats that were buried to the neck in the ground. This created a similar environment to a modern-day wine cellar. The Romans often left their pots open during this fermentation stage (about nine days) and would then seal them with clay or resin. The cheaper wines were used directly from the vats, but the higher quality were drawn off after a year into smaller jars (amphorae). Some of these better wines were clarified and enhanced with tree resin to prevent oxidation, and finally stored in storerooms often separate from the cellars.

Swirl, Sniff, and Savor

"Wine... the intellectual part of the meal."
—Alexander Dumas

What Would Jesus Drink?

I enjoyed writing the back of the bottle descriptions for the wines we made at Sharp's Hill Vineyards. I love the language of wine with its intrinsic richness from the vineyard experience to the winemaking in the cellar, and most of all drinking it for pleasure. I especially admire the expression of the flavors and aromatics it imparts. When it's well made, wine is poetry in a glass. It makes me wonder how I would approach a glass (or rather cup) of ancient wine and write a description of the taste, texture, and smell. It would surely be difficult to swirl in a clay or wooden cup. I especially wonder how Jesus would describe a modern California wine poured into an elegant, long-stemmed, clear wine glass. I think we would equally be rendered speechless.

The wine in general produced by the ancients was pretty strong and by today's standards quite unpalatable without enhancements. It really didn't taste very good on its own. This is one of the many reasons the ancient Romans mixed seawater with their wine before drinking it. This mixture tasted more like a spiked punch and resulted in reduced alcohol, so intoxication wasn't as easily achieved. It was a common practice to mix water with wine. Other additives were used in wine for various reasons, to sweeten it, honey was added, and they called it *muslum* wine, as was lead—this explains a lot— and spices and herbs were often infused for medicinal purposes (in addition to flavor). Scripture tells us it was good for the stomach, *"No longer drink only water, but use a little wine for the sake of your stomach and your frequent ailments"* (1 Timothy 5:23).

These early wine connoisseurs believed that properly aged wine was better, although wine was rarely kept for years in the first century. Only the very rich or the skilled could buy or create a wine that lasted for three years or more. Usually, wine was consumed the year it was made. Aged wine was often just two years old, and most *old* wine was only three years old. There were circumstances when wine was made to age for many years, some up to twenty-five and those in underground vessels for fifty.

"In vino veritas," is a Latin phrase penned by Pliny, the Elder, that means "In wine, there is truth." It suggests a person under the influence of alcohol is more likely to speak their hidden thoughts and desires. Pliny lived at the high point in the Roman Empire's history of wine which is around the time of Jesus. It has been estimated that every citizen was drinking the equivalent of one bottle of wine a day. The good news is they were not stumbling around in a drunken stupor all day because the wine was relatively weak as it was mixed with water, and the better news is that the alcohol in it killed the bacteria in the unclean drinking water of the time.

Every now and then Rob and I open an older bottle of wine from our cellar, to find it has some sediment—even though it was filtered. Ancient wine was not filtered so you would find sediment in the bottom of your cup. You would also taste the tree resin used both to stop oxidation and to seal the vessels; this would have imparted more than a hint of turpentine or cough syrup. This was not a desired effect, but they became accustomed to it. Serious winemakers became increasingly interested in the aroma of wine—so much so that they experimented with various ways of amplifying a wine's bouquet.

In southern Gaul, which is the modern-day Rhône region of France, the early viticulturists planted aromatic herbs such as lavender and thyme in the vineyards thinking that it would affect the flavor of the grapes. Today, Rhône wines are often described as having the aroma of lavender and thyme, and this is more than just a romantic idea, it's increasingly believed to be a matter of organic chemistry and a reflection of terroir. Another interesting practice was the storage of the clay vessels in a smoke chamber called a fumarium to add smokiness to a wine's flavor. Today, the use of heavily toasted barrels to add a hint of smokiness and other layers of toasted flavors achieves the same effect. Passum is another style of wine made from dried grapes or raisins, and was very much like a modern-day, Italian Amarone, which produces a very concentrated, rich wine.

Because wine didn't always taste good without enhancements, they found ways to make it not only more palatable, but in some cases sweeter, for instance they

What Would Jesus Pair?

would age wine on its lees (dead yeast cells), a practice we use today called *sur lie*, to make it softer and creamier. Chalk and marble dust were used to reduce acidity. Wines were often exposed to high temperatures, or even portions of it boiled to concentrate the sugars and added back in for flavor. Of course, the addition of honey from bees or dates, and herbs and spices like cinnamon or peppercorns would also do the trick. Wine was also made from fruit, particularly pomegranates and apples.

So much of what we know about ancient viticulture and winemaking comes from the works of many of the classical Roman writers, especially Virgil, Pliny, and Columella. Through their manuscripts we have learned how many of their techniques have influenced our modern winemaking practices. This includes how climate and landscape plays an important role in deciding which grape varieties to plant, the benefits of different trellising and vine-training systems, and the effects of pruning, thinning, and dropping fruit have on the quality of wine, as well as winemaking methods.

So, the question remains, *What would Jesus drink?*

At the time of Jesus, wine was at the center of ritual Jewish life as it is today; it holds a special place of importance in Jewish law and history. We know that the wine Jesus drank was kosher as required by Mosaic law, which means all the ingredients were required to be kosher. Grapes in their natural state are kosher, and any of the additives to make it more palatable would have to be as well.

Jesus drank all kinds of wine depending on where He was and who He was with. The early wines of Israel did not have a reputation for being the best tasting, but by the time of Jesus, winemaking had become creative and enhancements to make it taste better were not uncommon—as long as they were kosher. Jars have been found in Jerusalem dating back to the first century, with inscriptions indicating "from black raisins," "very dark," or "smokey." There is some indication that the wine of the Last Supper was rich and concentrated, and probably made with dried grapes in the style of our modern North-Italian Amarone. But unless we find the actual chalice Jesus used that night in the upper room—the Holy Grail, we will never know.

I asked my son Alec what kind of wine he thought Jesus would have liked best, red or white? I was astounded that he didn't hesitate with a very thoughtful answer. *"If Jesus loved all people equally, then He most likely loved all wine equally."* That's my boy! I asked Spencer the same question, and his answer was, *"Rosé, the best of both."*

Personally, I think Jesus was a red wine guy. The first reason is because there are so many great red wines that come from the Eastern Mediterranean—although the whites coming out of this region are delicious and pair well with the food. But mostly I think Jesus was a red guy because of the *cup* He offered *in remembrance* was *the new covenant in His blood*, and the bread His body. Despite this, I'm sure Jesus drank white wine too, and probably enjoyed it. The Romans preferred white wine, and mostly sweetened, however Jesus lived in the farthest corner of the Roman Empire, and evidence shows in the inscriptions on ancient vessels found that most of the wine from the Holy Land was in fact red.

The history of ancient wine reaches back to the beginning of time, and it embraces the history of Jesus every step of the way.

Section V

Passover is more than a time-honored Jewish tradition; it is commanded by God as a remembrance and sheds light on the Lord's Supper. Unpack the deeper connection between Jesus and the bread and wine at His table. Learn how to host your own Passover Seder celebration.

17

THE LORD'S SUPPER IN LIGHT OF PASSOVER

WHEN WE LIVED IN SOUTHERN California, we frequented the Festival of the Arts in Laguna Beach. Our favorite event was the Pageant of the Masters. This annual production, currently set in an outdoor, hillside amphitheater of the Laguna Canyon, has been a tradition since 1933. Ninety minutes of tableaux vivants—also known as living pictures—are recreated with real people in makeup and costumes posing to look like their counterparts in the original art works. Live narration, professional orchestra, sophisticated sets and lights make it a truly magical experience.

With few exceptions (only three since 1933), the program always ends with the world famous fifteenth-century painting of Leonardo da Vinci's, *Last Supper.*

This iconic painting, commissioned by the Dominican monastery Santa Maria delle Grazie in Milan, depicts Jesus and the disciples sitting around a rectangular table. Often, the walls of the room of monasteries, where nuns and monks ate their communal meals, were painted with scenes depicting Jesus and His disciples celebrating the Passover Seder. I wonder if it made those avowed *sisters* and *brothers* in dedicated servitude feel as if they were in the presence of their Lord Jesus for His *last supper*—the night before His crucifixion.

Da Vinci cleverly took artistic license and for the sake of vantage point, he placed the figures on one side of the table in the painting and interestingly each disciple is strategically seated in a special place in respective proximity to Jesus. It is rich with symbolism and foreshadowing; Judas will betray Him, Peter will deny Him (three times), and they all fall asleep even though Jesus had asked them to stay up with Him while He prayed in the Garden of Gethsemane. One important thing to observe is that the artist has Jesus gesturing toward a chalice of wine and a piece of bread—what would become the central elements in our Holy Communion, celebrating the Last Supper.

It is interesting that Da Vinci, among all the intended and strategic details of the scene, included a lot of food and wine on the table of this painting. Scripture tells us that Jesus and His twelve disciples went to Jerusalem and were in what we know as the upper room celebrating the festival of Passover—a Seder meal. They were not seated around a rectangular table, but rather they were reclining around a low, horseshoe-shaped table. The room was not depicted as it was in the masterpiece as a grand hall,

The Lord's Supper in Light of Passover

but instead a simple room. The food that was served was likely lamb stew, unleavened bread, olives, bitter herbs, and of course wine. The wine was not shared from a gold, jewel-encrusted chalice, but, surprising to most, a plain wooden cup. The disciples would have prepared their own Passover Seder meal under strict kosher law. The preparation and consumption of food was subject to particular restrictions that became the basis for Jewish dietary practices, many of which are still practiced today.

> *"Then they shall take some of the blood and put it on the two doorposts and the lintel of the houses in which they eat it. They shall eat the flesh that night, roasted on the fire; with unleavened bread and bitter herbs they shall eat it..."*—Exodus 12:7-8

The Jewish people have celebrated the Passover with a festive meal for thousands of years. Passover, also called Pesach, is a major holiday that recounts the Exodus of the Israelites from slavery in Egypt. It was intended, and still is today, to commemorate God's mercy for sparing them from the plague of the death of first-born sons in Egypt. This was the tenth and final plague. It marks the time when they were freed from slavery. The name Passover refers literally to the night when the angel of death "passed over" the houses of the Israelites whose door frames were painted in the blood of a sacrificed lamb and marked with a cross. This act set them apart and their children were spared, but the Egyptian children were not.

It was the Passover which prompted the exodus of the Hebrews from Egypt; they were freed from slavery—they were ransomed by God.

> *The Lord spoke to Moses, saying, "Speak to the people of Israel and say to them, These are the appointed feasts of the Lord that you shall proclaim as holy convocations; they are my appointed feasts."*—Leviticus 23:1-2

> *Passover was one of the three major festivals that had to be celebrated in Jerusalem within proximity of the Temple as mentioned in Leviticus 23 and Deuteronomy 16, and Jesus always traveled to Jerusalem for this occasion. In the first century, Jerusalem had a population of somewhere between 20,000 to 30,000 people, but the Holy City's population swelled by perhaps another 150,000 with the Jewish people who had traveled from throughout the world to celebrate.*[3]

Passover was a national pilgrimage and people started to arrive a week before to purify themselves. God commanded that all Jewish males be present in Jerusalem for the Passover (Exodus 23:17)—many of them brought

---

[3] Joachim Jeremias, *Jerusalem in the Time of Jesus* [Philadelphia: Fortress Press, 1969], p. 84.

The Lord's Supper in Light of Passover

their families. Imagine the intensity of multitudes of people and animals within the walls of the city all at one time. Nisan, in the Jewish calendar, is the first month of the year according to biblical calculation and usually falls within March and April. On the 14th day of Nisan, to commence the rites and rituals of Passover, thousands of lambs were sacrificially slaughtered by priests in a matter of just a few hours. This must have been overwhelmingly intense even for those who were used to it.

What must it have been like for Jesus at His final Passover as He witnessed the slaying of thousands of lambs and of the blood that was shed at the Temple? He knew His time had come and that He was establishing the New Passover by becoming *the* Sacrificial Lamb of the new covenant and that it would be His own blood that would fulfill the promise.

> "This day shall be for you a memorial day, and you shall keep it as a feast to the Lord; throughout your generations, as a statute forever, you shall keep it as a feast.
> —Exodus 12:14

Jesus was celebrating the Passover when He told His disciples that *He* was now the Sacrificial Lamb and that the bread He broke and the wine He shared signified His body and blood that would be shed. He specifically told them to eat and drink *in remembrance* of Him.

Why was it so important that the Apostle Paul recounted what Jesus told His disciples, "Do this in remembrance of me"? In the Jewish culture, as in many of the ancient cultures, storytelling was a means by which to hand down the traditions and teach their unique history to the next generations. Not everyone could read or had access to the Torah which is the first five books of the Old Testament known as the Pentateuch or Torah. The importance of Torah study has always been a hallmark for the Jews. It was, and still is, essential to their faith that they remember the Passover and all the stories in Exodus.

> *This shall be a day of remembrance for you. You shall celebrate it as a festival to the Lord; throughout your generations you shall observe it as a perpetual ordinance.*
> —Exodus 12:14

God established Passover to serve as a remembrance—a celebratory feast in remembrance of His gift of grace. It was a reminder to the Israelites of what He had done for them in the past, what He was doing at the present time, and pointed to what He would do in the future through Jesus. God always assured His people that He was with them always and would never leave them. Jesus, in celebrating the Passover, offered Himself. He said, "This *is* my body... this *is* my blood." The ordinary Passover Seder meal becomes extraordinary as we receive Jesus Himself

The Lord's Supper in Light of Passover

and His transformation in the upper room. That very night God delivered them as He had in the past, only this time with a new covenant—a new promise with new wine. — Pastor John Kunze - Sermon "In Remembrance"

> *The next day he saw Jesus coming toward him, and said, "Behold, the Lamb of God, who takes away the sin of the world!"* —John 1:29

The Exodus story required the blood of a lamb on the doorposts of the Israelites, but the new story of salvation required The Lamb—Jesus—who shed His own blood.

What did they eat and drink that night? What did they do? Looking at the final Passover Seder that Jesus and His twelve had celebrated in the upper room, it would have included some essential elements in that first-century meal. As mentioned earlier, there was likely lamb stew (a coincidence for the Lamb of God?), unleavened bread, bitter herbs, and wine. The kiddush—a special thanksgiving and prayer for the day of the feast was part of the ritual, and Hallel psalms were sung or recited. Most importantly, the story of the Exodus was told as a means of remembrance as commanded by God.

The wine and unleavened bread was and still is central to the Passover Seder. And as we know from the Gospels of Matthew, Mark, and Luke, the wine was in connection with the sacrament that Jesus instituted during Passover.

What Would Jesus Pair?

The Seder starts with first cup of wine and the blessing, *"Baruch Atah Adonai, Eloheinu Melech ha-olam, borei p'ree hagafen."* We praise God, Spirit of Everything, who creates the fruit of the vine.

The Bread and Wine of Passover

Four Cups of Wine

Not only does the Seder begin with a cup of wine but there are three additional wine blessings throughout. It's been established that these four cups of wine recall the four expressions of redemption that God commanded Moses to convey to the Jewish people. The four cups symbolize the freedoms from exile: the Hebrews were liberated from Pharaoh's four evil decrees:

- Slavery
- The ordered murder of all male descendants
- The drowning of all Hebrew boys in the Nile River
- Ordering the Israelites to collect their own straw to make bricks

The four cups also symbolize freedom from four exiles: the Egyptian, Babylonian, and Greek exiles, and the current exile which Jews hope to be rid of with the coming of the Messiah. Jews who believe that Jesus is the promised Messiah consider themselves already exiled. It's also interesting to note that the words "cup of wine" are mentioned four times in Pharaoh's butler's dream (Genesis 40:11-13). According to the Midrash (rabbinic biblical interpretation), these cups of wine alluded to the Israelites' liberation.

Basically, the four cups are meant to reflect the four phrases used in the Bible to describe God taking the Jews out of slavery. During the ritual, these phrases are spoken from Exodus 6:6-7:

- "I am the LORD, and **I will bring you** out from under the yoke of the Egyptians."
- "**I will deliver** you from their bondage."
- "**I will redeem** you with an outstretched arm and with great judgments."
- "Then **I will take** you as my people, and I will be your God; and you shall know that I am the Lord your God, who brought you out from under the burdens of the Egyptians."

Matzah

Matzah is unleavened bread that resembles a very large cracker. As a major part of the Passover Seder, it represents the bread that the Israelites took with them when they quickly fled Egypt—they didn't have time to leaven their bread. Consequently, it is considered the

What Would Jesus Pair?

bread of haste. It is made simply of flour and water (no yeast or shortening) and carries a greater meaning—freedom now! Matzah is the most emblematic food of Passover. It's also referred to as the bread of affliction, still today, the Jews relive the affliction of their ancestors with matzah in the Haggadah—the book or script that's read during the Seder and tells the story of Passover. And finally, matzah is considered the bread of unity—affliction can unite people in common empathy.

> *And they baked unleavened cakes of the dough that they had brought out of Egypt, for it was not leavened, because they were thrust out of Egypt and could not wait, nor had they prepared any provisions for themselves.*
> —Exodus 12:39

The Seder ritual includes a Matzah Tosch which is a pouch containing three layers of matzah. Early in the Seder, the head of the ritual removes the middle layer known as the afikoman, breaks it apart, and puts one broken half back in the middle; the other is hidden for the children to find later. The afikoman is seen symbolically in several ways: as their ultimate redemption from suffering; as a reference to the Passover sacrifice that used to be offered at the ancient temple in Jerusalem; as a reminder that the poor must always set something aside for the next meal;

The Lord's Supper in Light of Passover

or a reminder that there's always more to discover in life than what we know now.

Unleavened bread symbolizes both slavery and freedom—of leaving slavery behind and entering freedom—which is why, along with wine, it is central to the Passover Seder.

After the second cup of wine is presented, the cup of plagues, there is a feast. When taken together with a piece of the matzah that had been broken and hidden is found.

It is no coincidence that the third cup represents the Cup of Redemption. It is believed that it is the Cup of Redemption that Jesus told the disciples to drink from in the Last Supper. According to the Gospels, we see Matthew 26:27 and Luke 22:19 describing the cup being taken *after* the meal.

As the blood of the Passover Lamb covered the believing Israelites before they fled Egypt, so the blood of Christ covers Jewish and Christian believers today.

The bread that we break, is it not a participation in the body of Christ? Because there is one bread, we who are many are one body, for we all partake of the one bread.
—1 Corinthians 10:16-17

18

Observance of the Passover Seder

PASSOVER IS ONE OF THE most widely celebrated Jewish holidays even today. Rich with symbolism, it overflows with meaning and significance. The observance begins on the fifteenth day of the Jewish month of Nisan (late March or early April). It is a celebrated ritual enacted over seven days in Israel and for Reform Jews around the world, and for eight days for most other Jews outside of Israel. Conservative Jews follow these rituals carefully, though more progressive or Reform Jews may practice a more relaxed observance. The most important part of the ritual is the Passover meal, also known as the Seder.

According to Scripture, Jews are specifically commanded by God to retell the Exodus story. This usually takes place during the Passover Seder, which is a service of sorts held at home as part of the Passover celebration. The Seder is always observed on the first night of Passover and follows a series of fifteen steps, including a dinner of traditionally symbolic foods that are prepared on a Seder Plate. The telling of the Exodus story (the Magid) is the highlight of this event. It begins with the youngest person in the room asking four ceremonial questions and ends with a blessing recited over wine after the story is told—there is a lot that happens in between.

Passover is a kosher meal and the food is prepared and served under Jewish dietary laws. However, the rules of "kosher for Passover" are different from standard kosher rules. The most important kosher restriction for Passover is that leavened bread cannot be eaten—and actually no leavening is acceptable throughout Passover. This is where matzah comes in—the traditional unleavened bread. This custom originates from the Passover Exodus story when the Hebrew slaves fled Egypt so quickly that their bread didn't have time to rise. Eating matzah is an act of remembrance of the extreme haste when the Hebrews were forced to flee Egypt to freedom. For those partaking, it represents assuming a humble, subservient attitude and to be slave-like in the face of God.

Participants use a book or script called a Haggadah to lead the service, which consists of the Exodus storytelling, the ritualistic steps that lead up to a Seder meal, and the concluding prayers and songs. The word Haggadah comes from a Hebrew word meaning "tale" or "parable." The Haggadah contains an outline or choreography for the Seder. The word Seder means "order" in Hebrew.

Observance of the Passover Seder

Steps of the Passover Seder

The fifteen steps of the Passover Seder are observed strictly in some homes, while others may choose to observe only some of them and focus instead on the Passover Seder meal. Many Jewish families observe these steps according to long-standing tradition. In looking for just the right Haggadah to share, I learned that there are literally over 7,000 distinct versions printed. The dilemma was which one to use; I learned that many people choose one based on tradition and desire. A short Messianic Haggadah script, suggested Seder meal and recipes are included in this section if you choose to host your own Passover Seder. Here is an overview that outlines the fifteen basic steps.

1. Kadesh (Sanctification)

The Seder meal begins with kiddush (a ceremony of prayer and blessing over the wine) and the first of four cups of wine that will be enjoyed during the Seder. Each participant's cup is filled with wine (or grape juice) and the blessing is recited aloud, then everyone takes a drink from their cup while leaning to the left. (Leaning is a way of showing freedom, because, in ancient times, only free people reclined while eating.)

2. Urchatz (Purification/Handwashing)

Water is poured over the hands to symbolize ritual purification. Traditionally, a special handwashing cup is used to pour water over the right hand first, then the left. On any other day of the year, Jews say a blessing called netilat yadayim during the handwashing ritual, but on Passover, no blessing is said, prompting the children to ask, "*Why is this night different from all other nights?*"

3. Karpas (Appetizer)

A blessing is recited over a vegetable such as lettuce, cucumber, radish, or parsley is dipped in salt water and eaten. The salt water represents the tears of the Israelites that were shed during their years of enslavement in Egypt.

4. Yachatz (Breaking the Matzah)

There is always a plate of three matzot (plural of matzah) stacked on the table—often on a special matzah tray—during a Seder meal, in addition to extra matzah for the guests to eat during the meal. At this point, the Seder leader takes the middle matzah and breaks it in half. The smaller piece is then put back between the remaining two matzot. The larger half becomes the afikomen, which is placed in an afikomen bag or wrapped in a napkin and is hidden somewhere in the house for the children to find at the end of the Seder meal. Alternatively, some homes place the afikomen near the Seder leader and the children must try to "steal" it without the leader noticing.

5. Maggid (Telling the Passover Story)

During this part of the Seder, the Seder plate is moved aside, the second cup of wine is poured, and participants retell the Exodus story. A Seder plate has wells in it to hold the symbolic food items that are referenced and used during the ritual. The placement and symbolism of the items on this special plate is important.

The youngest person (usually a child) at the table begins by asking the *Four Questions*. Each question is a variation of: *"Why is this night different from all other nights?"* Participants will often answer these questions by taking turns reading from the Haggadah. Next, the four types of children are described: the wise child, the wicked child, the simple child, and the child who doesn't know how to ask a question. Thinking about each kind of person is an opportunity for self-reflection and discussion.

As each of the ten plagues that struck Egypt is read aloud from Scripture, participants dip a finger (usually the pinky) into their wine and put a drop of liquid onto their plates. At this point, the various symbols on the Seder plate are discussed, and then everyone drinks their wine.

6. Rachtzah (Handwashing Before the Meal)

Participants wash their hands again, this time saying the appropriate netilat yadayim blessing. After saying the blessing, it is customary not to speak until the recitation of the ha'motzi blessing over the matzah.

7. Motzi (Blessing for the Matzah)

While holding the three matzot, the leader recites the ha'motzi blessing for bread. The leader then places the bottom matzah back on the table or matzah tray and, while holding the top whole matzah and the broken middle matzah, recites the blessing mentioning the mitzvah (commandment) to eat matzah. The leader breaks pieces from each of these two pieces of matzah and provides for everyone at the table to eat.

8. Matzah

Everyone eats their matzah.

9. Maror (Bitter Herbs)

Because the Israelites were slaves in Egypt, Jews eat bitter herbs as a reminder of the harshness of servitude. Horseradish, either the root or a prepared paste, is most often used, although many have taken on the custom of using the bitter parts of romaine lettuce dipped into charoset, a paste made of apples and nuts. Customs vary from community to community. The latter is shaken off before the recitation of the commandment to eat bitter herbs.

10. Korech (Hillel Sandwich)

Next, participants make and eat the "Hillel Sandwich" by putting maror and charoset between two pieces of matzah broken off the last whole matzah, the bottom matzah.

11. Shulchan Orech (Dinner)

At last, it's time for the meal to begin. The Passover Seder meal usually begins with a hard-boiled egg dipped in salt water. Then, the rest of the lavish meal features dishes such as matzah ball soup, beef brisket, and even matzah lasagna in some communities. Dessert often includes ice cream, cheesecake, or flourless chocolate cakes.

12. Tzafun (Eating the Afikomen)

After dessert, participants eat the afikomen. Remember that the afikomen was either hidden or stolen at the beginning of the Seder meal, so it has to be returned to the Seder leader at this point. In some homes, the children actually negotiate with the Seder leader for treats or toys before giving the afikomen back.

After eating the afikomen, which is considered the Seder meal's "dessert," no other food or drink is consumed, except for the last two cups of wine.

13. Barech (Blessings After the Meal)

The third cup of wine is poured for everyone, the blessing is recited, and then participants drink their glass. Then, an additional cup of wine is poured for Elijah in a special cup called Elijah's Cup, and a door is opened so that the prophet can enter the home. For some families, a special Miriam's Cup is also poured at this point.

14. Hallel (Songs of Praise)

The door is closed, and everyone sings songs of praise to God before drinking the fourth and final cup of wine while reclining.

15. Nirtzah (Acceptance)

The Seder is now officially over, but most homes recite one final blessing: L'shanah haba'ah b'Yerushalayim! This means, "Next year in Jerusalem!" and expresses the hope that next year, all Jews will celebrate Passover in Israel.[4]

---

[4] Ariela Pelaia, "The Order and Meaning of the Passover Seder," Learn Religions, Aug. 28, 2020, learnreligions.com/what-is-a-passover-seder-2076456.

19

A Passover Meal and Menu

DURING MY COLLEGE DAYS IN Philadelphia, I had a roommate, Melanie, who was Jewish. I had never experienced the Jewish culture as it pertained to the religious holidays and respective culinary traditions. The first year we lived together, she broke out the matzah bread, Jarlsberg cheese, and Manischewitz wine during Passover (all of which are kosher). I was pretty clueless as to the Passover traditions, but I loved snacking on those unleavened crackers with cheese, and the wine. The iconic Manischewitz wine is made in New York from Concord grapes. Concord grapes are not really wine grapes as they have an entirely different profile. So, needless to say, this traditional Passover beverage is more like grape juice with 11 percent alcohol, it is very sweet.

Later, when I was in my mid-thirties, I moved to California and worked with a Jewish girl from New Jersey who became a close friend. Nadine and her family always included us in the Jewish feasts, and we became part of their extended family and fond of the traditional food—syrupy-sweet Manischewtiz wine notwithstanding. Potato

What Would Jesus Pair?

latkes with applesauce or sour cream, chicken matzah ball soup, and beef brisket were among our favorites. The best part was that they always sent us home with more leftovers than we could ever eat. I even liked the gefilte fish with horseradish. Their matzah ball soup rivaled that of the Latimer Delicatessen in Philadelphia, and Jerry's Famous Deli in Southern California—both extraordinary Jewish delis.

Over the past forty years since I first encountered it, I have become fond of classic Jewish food and have come to realize the Passover traditions are many and vary by region and culture. Most American Passover traditions come from the 80 percent of Jews who trace their roots to Eastern and Central Europe. My personal experience is significantly based on American non-religious traditions. As I researched international Passover food, I found the options were endless (the same plight I had when searching for the right Haggadah). As Jews have scattered around the world over thousands of years, their respective cuisine has evolved with time and according to their cultural customs. Despite the differences, one thing that is the same for every Jewish family celebrating the Passover Seder is that it starts at sundown on the same date and that it was commanded by God.

The variation of Seder customs worldwide is fascinating. These are just some of the unique practices from around the globe: in Morocco, they invite neighbors over

A Passover Meal and Menu

to eat sweets; in Poland, they re-enact the crossing of the Red Sea, in Syria they break Matzah into the shape of Hebrew letters, and in Iran and Afghanistan they gently whack each other with bunches of scallions. The food is diverse as well. In Northern Africa, dates are in abundance, in Eastern Europe variations of borscht (beet soup) and beet dishes are prevalent, in South Africa apples are a featured ingredient, and a popular side dish in Rome is fried artichokes.

Some people think serving lamb is synonymous with Passover. Surprisingly, you won't usually see lamb on the table at your average Jewish Passover Seder. While it is appropriate for some to serve lamb for Passover, the rules that govern the preparation are subject to differing interpretations, therefore most Seder dinners forgo it. The ancient custom of sacrificing lambs on the night before Passover and eating the roasted meat to begin the festival ended with the destruction of the Second Temple in AD 70. The Torah's commands could not be met without a temple. And without question it is no coincidence that Jesus had fulfilled the sacrificial requirement of a spotless lamb, whose blood was shed once and for all. *"For Christ, our Passover lamb, has been sacrificed"* (1 Corinthians 5:7).

Regardless of culture and custom, the variety of Passover food is endless. Many foods are designated specifically for Passover, but many foods that are not unique to this special meal can be eaten providing kosher guidelines for handling and the ingredients are followed for those wishing to remain kosher. If you are not Jewish and simply want to experience a Seder meal, kosher guidelines are not an issue. I truly had a hard time narrowing down my suggestion of recipes for a DIY Seder dinner; the food is all so delicious. While I am providing a menu with different options for the courses (based on my desires), there is a world of Passover recipes out there to explore. There's a dish for every taste, style, and preference including vegetarian and vegan.

A note about the wine: There are four cups of wine referenced and consumed during the Seder observance if you are going to use the traditional Haggadah script. While I prefer a dryer red wine as I'll serve beef brisket, please feel free to drink whatever wine you like, red, white, or even Manischewitz. And yes, grape juice, or better yet pomegranate juice is a good substitute for children and those who do not wish to imbibe. And you don't have to fill your wine glass to the brim, not unless you want to.

Shulchan Orech—Let's Eat

The Passover Seder meal usually begins with a hard-boiled egg dipped in salt water. As I mentioned before, the rest of the lavish meal features matzah ball soup, beef brisket, and even matzah lasagna in some communities. Dessert often includes ice cream, cheesecake, or flourless chocolate cakes.

A Passover Meal and Menu

The Passover menu I have suggested is based on more traditional dishes you would likely find at a Seder with my own personal twist. Pick and choose from these offerings, and if you have a favorite recipe you'd prefer, or in addition to what I have suggested, go for it. Most Passover Seder dinners are as unique as the family celebrating it. As for the wine, I say drink what you like, but if you are excited to try something new and to have a meaningful experience, I suggest trying Israeli wine—it's reminiscent of the Holy Land. Ask your local wine merchant if they can make recommendations and order it for you. Israel boasts over 300 wineries ranging from small boutique to very large commercial production.

Be adventurous. L'chaim!

Enjoy these tried and true Passover dishes.

- Roasted Beet Salad with Goat Cheese, page 286
- Chicken Matzah Ball Soup, page 279
- Beef Brisket, page 312
- Lemony Herb Roasted Chicken, page 309
- Charoset Salad, page 290
- Apple Matzah Potato Kugel, page 298
- Barley Roasted Mediterranean Vegetables, page 292
- Wine Poached Pears, page 316
- Flourless Chocolate Cake, page 319
- Doctored up Gefilte Fish,* page 275

*If you want to take adventure to a new level, try gefilte fish with or without horseradish. I know, it sounds scary, but you might just be pleasantly surprised as I was. While homemade is best, there is an easy alternative to doctor up gefilte fish from a jar, especially if this is a first for you. I cannot take credit for this recipe because I have not had much experience with this unique dish, but this trick is easy and actually does the jar of fish justice.

20

A SHORT FAMILY MESSIANIC HAGGADAH

THIS MESSIANIC FAMILY HAGGADAH IS designed for use with your family, home group, or church to celebrate a Jesus-centered Passover Seder. Enjoy this shorter version of the Haggadah in which Christians, and Jews who believe Jesus is the Messiah, will find appropriate to their faith and rich in symbolism.

Often, the Bible readings are read by the leader, but guests can also participate. In ancient times a cup of wine was divided between guests, which led to the tradition of four cups at the Seder, along with their individual meaning. Drinking four full, separate glasses of wine is not necessary, but be prepared with plenty of wine. Passover should be celebrated with great joy, so please feel free to make this special meal, including the Haggadah, unique to your family.

Jesus is mentioned by name in this version. Many Messianic or Christian scripts refer to Him using the name *Yeshua*. I have also included several of the blessings throughout in Hebrew and English if you wish to enjoy the traditional language as well. While Jesus spoke Aramaic

What Would Jesus Pair?

and His Passover Seder would have been in that language, He also understood Hebrew.

While the ancient Jews celebrating the Passover were reclining on a low table, you do not have to. But I suggest you lean to the left when drinking each cup of wine as part of the ritual.

Ingredients and Necessary Items

- A Seder Plate or a plate large enough to hold all six items (lamb shank bone, egg, parsley, piece of horseradish, creamed horseradish sauce, charoset)
- A bowl and pitcher of water for hand washing
- Hand towels
- A box of matzah
- An afikomen bag (a cloth or silk bag containing three compartments, each holding a piece of matzah; if you can't obtain a bag, four cloth napkins can be used as an alternative)
- A lamb shank bone (if lamb is hard to find, use a beef shank bone from your butcher)
- A hard-boiled egg
- Fresh Parsley
- Dish of salt water
- Creamed horseradish sauce
- A piece of horseradish
- Charoset (see end of chapter for recipe)
- Two tapered candles in candlesticks and matches

- Red wine of your choice—everyone starts with a glass of wine
- Grape juice (for children and those who don't want to drink alcohol)
- Reward for the child who finds the afikomen (candy, tiny toys, or coins)

The Seder Begins

While the leader reads all of the Bible verses including the 10 plagues, you may share some or all of the readings.

Washing One Another's Hands

Leader: *Welcome to our Passover meal. This will be a Messianic Seder, which means it will honor Jesus the Messiah, Yeshua haMashiach, as the true Passover lamb. We'll begin with the traditional washing of hands.* [The best way to do this is to pass around a deep bowl, a pitcher of water, and a hand towel. The bowl is placed in front of one person while the person on the right pours a little water from the pitcher over the first person's hands, which are held over the bowl, then they dry their hands on the towel. Then the bowl moves to the left and so on until everyone's hands are washed.]

What Would Jesus Pair?

Leader: *It was at this point in the meal that Jesus washed the feet of His disciples. Our first Bible reading is from John Chapter 13, verses 3 to 17:*

Jesus, knowing that the Father had given all things into his hands, and that he had come from God and was going back to God, rose from supper. He laid aside his outer garments, and taking a towel, tied it around his waist. Then he poured water into a basin and began to wash the disciples' feet and to wipe them with the towel that was wrapped around him. He came to Simon Peter, who said to him, "Lord, do you wash my feet?" Jesus answered him, "What I am doing you do not understand now, but afterward you will understand." Peter said to him, "You shall never wash my feet." Jesus answered him, "If I do not wash you, you have no share with me." Simon Peter said to him, "Lord, not my feet only but also my hands and my head!" Jesus said to him, "The one who has bathed does not need to wash, except for his feet, but is completely clean. And you are clean, but not every one of you." For he knew who was to betray him; that was why he said, "Not all of you are clean." When he had washed their feet and put on his outer garments and resumed his place, he said to them, "Do you understand what I have done to you? You call me Teacher and Lord, and you are right, for so I am. If I then, your Lord and Teacher, have washed your feet, you also ought to wash one another's feet. For I have given you an example, that you also should do just as I have done to you. Truly, truly, I say to you, a servant is not greater than his master, nor is a messenger greater than the one who sent him. *If you know these things, blessed are you if you do them.*

Lighting of the Candles

The candles are lit by the woman of the house, while doing so says: *Baruch Atah Adonai Eloheinu melech ha'olam asher kid'shanu b'mitzvotav, v'tzivanu l'hadlik ner shel Shabbat V'shel Yom Tov. Blessed are You, Adonai our God, Ruler of the Universe, who has sanctified us with laws and commanded us to light Shabbat lights and the festival lights. As we light the festival candles, we acknowledge that as they brighten our Passover table, good thoughts, good words, and good deeds brighten our days.*

The Question of the Youngest Child

Child (or Youngest Person): *Why is this night different from all other nights?*

Leader: *It is because of what the Lord our God did for us when we came out of Egypt. With a mighty hand the Lord brought us out of Egypt, out of the land of slavery. When Pharaoh, king of Egypt, stubbornly refused to let us go, the Lord killed every firstborn in Egypt, both man and animal. But he passed over the houses of the Israelites in Egypt and spared our homes. That is why it is called the Passover. The Lord commanded us to commemorate the Passover for the generations to come as a festival to the Lord. At Passover we eat unleavened bread, because the Israelites* did not have time to add yeast to their dough on the night when they were driven out of Egypt.

The First Cup of Wine—Kiddush (Cup of Sanctification)

The leader says a blessing, just as Jesus Himself did at this stage in the Last Supper.

Leader: [Hold up the first cup]. *This first cup is the Kiddush, the cup of Sanctification. Baruch Atah Adonai, Eloheinu Melech ha-olam, borei p'ree hagafen. Blessed are you, Lord our God, King of the Universe, who created the fruit of the vine.* [Everyone leans left and drinks from their own glass].

Leader: *Our next Bible reading is from Luke Chapter 22, verses 14-18:*

And when the hour came, he reclined at table, and the apostles with him. And he said to them, "I have earnestly desired to eat this Passover with you before I suffer. For I tell you I will not eat it until it is fulfilled in the kingdom of God." And he took a cup, and when he had given thanks he said, "Take this, and divide it among yourselves. For I tell you that from now on I will not drink of the fruit of the vine until the kingdom of God comes."

The Second Cup of Wine—the Cup of Plagues (Deliverance)

Leader: [Hold up the second cup]. *The Bible commands us not to gloat over the misfortune of our enemies, and so by way of solemn remembrance while the ten plagues are recited, each person uses a finger to spill ten drops of wine on his or her plate, one per plague as the Scripture is read.* [Everyone leans left and drinks from their own glass].

The leader reads the following passages or arranges for guests to read them.

Leader:

The First Plague—Blood

Then the Lord said to Moses, "Pharaoh's heart is hardened; he refuses to let the people go. Go to Pharaoh in the morning, as he is going out to the water. Stand on the bank of the Nile to meet him, and take in your hand the staff that turned into a serpent. And you shall say to him, 'The Lord, the God of the Hebrews, sent me to you, saying, "Let my people go, that they may serve me in the wilderness." But so far, you have not obeyed. Thus says the Lord, "By this you shall know that I am the Lord: behold, with the staff that is in my hand I will strike the water that is in the Nile, and it shall turn into blood. The fish in the Nile shall die, and the Nile will stink, and the Egyptians will grow weary of drinking water from the Nile."'" (Exodus 7:14-18)

The Second Plague—Frogs

Then the Lord said to Moses, "Go in to Pharaoh and say to him, 'Thus says the Lord, "Let my people go, that they may serve me. But if you refuse to let them go, behold, I will plague all your country with frogs. The Nile shall swarm with frogs that shall come up into your house and into your bedroom and on your bed and into the houses of your servants and your people, and into your ovens and your kneading bowls. The frogs shall come up on you and on your people and on all your servants."'" (Exodus 8:1-4)

The Third Plague—Gnats

Then the Lord said to Moses, "Say to Aaron, 'Stretch out your staff and strike the dust of the earth, so that it may become gnats in all the land of Egypt.'" And they did so. Aaron stretched out his hand with his staff and struck the dust of the earth, and there were gnats on man and beast. All the dust of the earth became gnats in all the land of Egypt. (Exodus 8:16-17)

The Fourth Plague—Flies

Then the Lord said to Moses, "Rise up early in the morning and present yourself to Pharaoh, as he goes out to the water, and say to him, 'Thus says the Lord, "Let my people go, that they may serve me. Or else, if you will not let my people go, behold, I will send swarms of flies on you and your servants and your people, and into your houses. And the houses of the Egyptians shall be filled with swarms of flies, and also the ground on which they stand."'" (Exodus 8:20-21)

The Fifth Plague—Livestock

Then the Lord said to Moses, "Go in to Pharaoh and say to him, 'Thus says the Lord, the God of the Hebrews, "Let my people go, that they may serve me. For if you refuse to let them go and still hold them, behold, the hand of the Lord will fall with a very severe plague upon your livestock that are in the field, the horses, the donkeys, the camels, the herds, and the flocks. But the Lord will make a distinction between the livestock of Israel and the livestock of Egypt, so that nothing of all that belongs to the people of Israel shall die."'" And the Lord set a time, saying, "Tomorrow the Lord will do this thing in the land." And the next day the Lord did this thing. All the livestock of the Egyptians died, but not one of the livestock of the people of Israel died. And Pharaoh sent, and behold, not one of the livestock of Israel was dead. But the heart of Pharaoh was hardened, and he did not let the people go. (Exodus 9:1-7)

The Sixth Plague—Boils

And the Lord said to Moses and Aaron, "Take handfuls of soot from the kiln, and let Moses throw them in the air in the sight of Pharaoh. It shall become fine dust over all the land of Egypt, and become boils breaking out in sores on man and beast throughout all the land of Egypt." (Exodus 9:8-9)

The Seventh Plague—Hail

Then the Lord said to Moses, "Rise up early in the morning and present yourself before Pharaoh and say to him, 'Thus says the Lord, the God of the Hebrews, "Let my people go, that they may serve me. For this time I will send all my plagues on you yourself, and on your servants and your people, so that you may know that there is none like me in all the earth. For by now I could have put out my hand and struck you and your people with pestilence, and you would have been cut off from the earth. But for this purpose I have raised you up, to show you my power, so that my name may be proclaimed in all the earth. You are still exalting yourself against my people and will not let them go. Behold, about this time tomorrow I will cause very heavy hail to fall, such as never has been in Egypt from the day it was founded until now. Now therefore send, get your livestock and all that you have in the field into safe shelter, for every man and beast that is in the field and is not brought home will die when the hail falls on them.""" Then whoever feared the word of the Lord among the servants of Pharaoh hurried his slaves and his livestock into the houses, but whoever did not pay attention to the word of the Lord left his slaves and his livestock in the field. (Exodus 9:13-21)

A Short Family Messianic Haggadah

The Eighth Plague—Locusts

So Moses and Aaron went in to Pharaoh and said to him, "Thus says the Lord, the God of the Hebrews, 'How long will you refuse to humble yourself before me? Let my people go, that they may serve me. For if you refuse to let my people go, behold, tomorrow I will bring locusts into your country, and they shall cover the face of the land, so that no one can see the land. And they shall eat what is left to you after the hail, and they shall eat every tree of yours that grows in the field.'" (Exodus 10:3-5)

The Ninth Plague—Darkness

Then the Lord said to Moses, "Stretch out your hand toward heaven, that there may be darkness over the land of Egypt, a darkness to be felt." So Moses stretched out his hand toward heaven, and there was pitch darkness in all the land of Egypt three days. They did not see one another, nor did anyone rise from his place for three days, but all the people of Israel had light where they lived. (Exodus 10:21-23)

The Tenth Plague—The Firstborn Sons

The Lord said to Moses, "Yet one plague more I will bring upon Pharaoh and upon Egypt. Afterward he will let you go from here. When he lets you go, he will drive you away completely. Speak now in the hearing of the people, that they ask, every man of his neighbor and every woman of her neighbor, for silver and gold jewelry." And the Lord gave the people favor in the sight of the Egyptians. Moreover, the man Moses was very great in

What Would Jesus Pair?

the land of Egypt, in the sight of Pharaoh's servants and in the sight of the people. So Moses said, "Thus says the Lord: 'About midnight I will go out in the midst of Egypt, and every firstborn in the land of Egypt shall die, from the firstborn of Pharaoh who sits on his throne, even to the firstborn of the slave girl who is behind the handmill, and all the firstborn of the cattle. There shall be a great cry throughout all the land of Egypt, such as there has never been, nor ever will be again. But not a dog shall growl against any of the people of Israel, either man or beast, that you may know that the Lord makes a distinction between Egypt and Israel.' And all these your servants shall come down to me and bow down to me, saying, 'Get out, you and all the people who follow you.' And after that I will go out." And he went out from Pharaoh in hot anger. Then the Lord said to Moses, "Pharaoh will not listen to you, that my wonders may be multiplied in the land of Egypt." Moses and Aaron did all these wonders before Pharaoh, and the Lord hardened Pharaoh's heart, and he did not let the people of Israel go out of his land. The Lord said to Moses and Aaron in the land of Egypt, "This month shall be for you the beginning of months. It shall be the first month of the year for you. Tell all the congregation of Israel that on the tenth day of this month every man shall take a lamb according to their fathers' houses, a lamb for a household. And if the household is too small for a lamb, then he and his nearest neighbor shall take according to the number of persons; according to what each can eat you shall make your count for the lamb. Your lamb shall be without blemish, a male a year old. You may take it from the sheep or from the goats, and you shall keep it until the fourteenth day of this month, when the whole assembly of the congregation of Israel shall kill their lambs at twilight. Then they shall take some of the blood and put it on the two doorposts and the lintel of the houses in which they eat it. They shall eat the flesh that night, roasted on the fire; with unleavened bread and bitter herbs they shall eat it. Do not eat any of it raw or boiled in water, but roasted, its head with its legs and its inner parts. And you shall let none of it remain until the morning; anything that remains until the morning you shall burn. In this manner you shall eat it: with your belt fastened, your sandals on your feet, and your staff in your hand. And you shall eat it in haste. It is the Lord's Passover. For I will pass through the land of Egypt that night, and I will strike all the firstborn in the land of Egypt, both man and beast; and on all the gods of Egypt I will execute judgments: I am the Lord. The blood shall be a sign for you, on the houses where you are. And when I see the blood, I will pass over you, and no plague will befall you to destroy you, when I strike the land of Egypt." (Exodus 11:1-10; 12:1-13)*

The Hiding of the Afikomen

At this point the matzah in the middle of the three compartments of the afikomen bag is removed and broken in two. One of its pieces is placed in a cloth napkin and hidden by the leader. When the meal is over, the children will search for it and bring it back for a reward. Meanwhile matzah (not from the afikomen bag) is given to everyone at the table to eat with the items on the Seder plate.

The Seder Plate

This traditionally holds six items: parsley, a boiled egg, a lamb shank bone, bitter herbs (usually creamed horseradish), a piece of horseradish, and charoset. The leader will introduce each one with a description as they appear in the script.

Leader: *First, the parsley.* [The leader dips this in a bowl of salt water and then shakes it in view of everyone at the table]. *The drops from the parsley symbolize the tears of the Israelites during their enslavement in Egypt.*

Leader: *Second the egg. The egg is a symbol of mourning that reminds us of the destruction of the temple in AD 70. The temple's destruction is the reason why Jewish people never sacrifice a lamb at Passover, despite the Bible's directions.*

Leader: *Third, the shank bone. This dry bone takes the place of a sacrificed lamb, because without the temple no sacrifices can lawfully be made. As followers of Jesus, we believe that He is the true Passover Lamb. He was slain in our place. Anyone who trusts in His atoning blood receives forgiveness of sins. It is as if His blood is on the doorframe of our lives, and the Lord will pass over us when He punishes the wicked on His day of justice.*

Leader: *Fourth and fifth, the bitter herbs.* [There is a ceremonial piece of horseradish on the Seder plate, but the creamed horseradish is passed around and eaten by guests with matzah]. *We eat these bitter herbs to remind us of the harshness of slavery in Egypt.*

Leader: *Sixth, charoset.* [This too is passed around and eaten with matzah by each guest]. *The charoset resembles the mortar that the Israelite slaves used as they labored on building projects in Egypt.*

The Meal

The main meal is now served. This is a great time to enjoy one another's company and conversation—and wine of course—while you eat.

The Search for the Afikomen

After the meal, the children search for the hidden afikomen. Once it has been found and returned for a reward, the leader breaks it into small pieces and gives one to everyone at the table to eat. If there are no children present at your dinner, then by all means let your inner child take part in the fun.

Leader: *Our next Bible reading is Luke Chapter 22, verse 19:*

And he took bread, and when he had given thanks, he broke it and gave it to them, saying, "This is my body, which is given for you. Do this in remembrance of me."

The Third Cup of Wine—the Cup of Blessing

Leader: [Hold up the third cup]. *The third cup of wine is the cup of blessing, also known as the cup of redemption. This is the cup spoken of by the Apostle Paul:*

In the same way also he took the cup, after supper, saying, "This cup is the new covenant in my blood. Do this, as often as you drink it, in remembrance of me." For as often as you eat this bread and drink the cup, you proclaim the Lord's death until he comes. (1 Corinthians 11:25-26) [Everyone leans left and drinks from their own cup].

The Fourth Cup of Wine—Hallel

Leader: [Hold up the fourth cup]. *This is the cup of Hallel, which means "praise." Baruch Atah Adonai, Eloheinu Melech ha-olam, borei p'ree hagafen. We praise God, Ruler of Everything, who creates the fruit of the vine.* [Lean left and everyone drink the fourth and final glass of wine]!

A Short Family Messianic Haggadah

Leader: *We close our Seder by saying, "L'Shanah Haba'ah B'Yerushalyim", which means "Next Year in Jerusalem." For centuries, this declaration expressed the Jewish people's goal to return to our homeland. Even after the founding of the State of Israel in 1948, these words still resonate with the Jewish people.*

Shalom

Note: Traditional Jewish families would sing songs after dinner that praise God. If you choose to do this, I suggest ending with the doxology—or the Hymn of Praise:

Praise God from whom all blessings flow
Praise Him, all creatures here below
Praise Him above, ye Heavenly host
Praise Father, Son, and Holy Ghost
Amen

Passover Charoset

(Serve with Matzah as part of the Seder, and as a side dish during the meal.)

INGREDIENTS

> 6 medium (firm) apples, such as Fuji or Honeycrisp, peeled and finely diced
> 2 c. toasted walnuts, roughly chopped
> 1/2 c. golden raisins
> 1/2 c. sweet red wine
> 1 tbsp. honey
> 2 tsp. lemon zest
> 2 tsp. ground cinnamon
> Pinch kosher salt

Mix all ingredients in a bowl until well combined. Let set for at least 30 minutes before serving. Serves 8

21

Conclusion

For he satisfies the longing soul, and the hungry soul he fills with good things. —Psalm 107:9

THIS BOOK YOU HOLD IN your hand is not exactly the book I originally set out to write. It is so much more. What was to be a first-century epicurean travelog of Jesus and the disciples became a deeper dive into what the people of Scripture ate and why. It took me back through the far reaches of time where it all began at creation. It is an exploration of the biblical culinary world spanning thousands of years.

It's no secret that the Bible is filled to the brim with vivid imagery of food, feasts, vineyards, and wine from the beginning of time to the end. In the beginning God planted the most magnificent garden to feed and sustain His creation; in the very end a fruit-bearing tree stands at the center of His magnificent story and evokes images of the Garden of Eden where God had originally placed mankind. Like the rhythm of the seasons, everything comes full circle.

What Would Jesus Pair?

The Gospel of John opens with these words, *"In the beginning was the Word, and the Word was with God, and the Word was God. He was in the beginning with God."* (John 1:1-2) Jesus was there in the beginning—Father, Son, and Holy Spirit.

The Bible continues on from the Garden of Eden through the centuries of religious rites and rituals, the feasts and banquets, cultural traditions and events that led up to the life and times of Jesus. I became acutely aware that the culinary culture of the first century could not be isolated, but instead examined with a deeper understanding of the history that pre-dated Jesus' ministry on earth.

The story of humankind, and how God sustained them physically and spiritually since the beginning, is a true love story. We know this because every good and perfect gift is from above.

As Jesus and the disciples traveled throughout the Eastern Mediterranean, each region offered up a unique array of fruits and vegetables, fish, foul, and livestock for meat and dairy. The food they prepared was accentuated by herbs and spices, and the variety of wines spoke of the respective terroir—that certain sense of place. These would encompass the food and wine Jesus would have experienced—what would inevitably have been "paired" at every meal.

All the while, I imagined being side-by-side with Jesus and the disciples joining in the preparation of a

CONCLUSION

meal, conversations about the people and circumstances encountered, and learning from our beloved Rabbi over a cup of wine. It made me wonder, if in those moments, did the disciples truly grasp the significance of what was transpiring—they were in the presence of and sharing life with the *Son of God*.

While I have always had a passion for good food and wine, the significance of breaking bread together and sharing a meal took on a new meaning. Food and wine plays a central role in our relationship with God and with one another. Jesus declared, *"I am the Bread of Life,"* and *"I am the Vine."* He offered His body and blood to save us; at the Lord's Supper, we are united. We are connected to one another through the culinary experience—we are connected to Jesus through the bread and wine at His table.

> *On this mountain the Lord of hosts will make for all peoples a feast of rich food, a feast of well-aged wine, of rich food full of marrow, of aged wine well refined.*
> —Isaiah 25:6

Imagine dining at an endless table laid with the most scrumptious delights the earth has to offer, and gleaming wine goblets brimming with a heavenly vintage. God desires to nurture and richly feed His people.

A meal is elevated by a lofty loaf of crusty bread and a bottle of handcrafted wine. I pray that you have been inspired to celebrate even the simplest meals making it a sacred time and blessed occasion to share with family and friends. Know that food and wine is God's language of love. It nourishes our very body and soul.

> *Drinking good wine with good food in good company is one of life's most civilized [and sacred] pleasures.*
> —Michael Broadbent

Section VI

"A recipe has no soul. You, as the cook, must bring the soul to the recipe." —Thomas Keller

ARMED WITH AN UNDERSTANDING OF the traditions of the Bible, as well as the food and wine Jesus would have celebrated, it's time to get cooking. These are not first-century recipes, but instead dishes that honor the traditions, flavors, and nuance of the Mediterranean and its influence on modern cuisine.

Grab your spoon and stir up some of these carefully selected recipes with modern wine pairing suggestions, make them your own, and try to imagine...

What Would Jesus Pair?

Bon Appetit!

22

THE ART OF PAIRING

Food and wine. Decide which is the soloist, which the accompanist. —Michael Broadbent

THERE IS NOTHING QUITE AS delightful as when food and wine are perfectly paired. The movie, Ratatouille, exemplifies the art pairing in the most playful way. In this delightful animated film set in Paris, an unlikely rat named Remy lives out his culinary passion. When he tastes food in combinations, and with herbs and spices, it's like a symphony being performed in his senses, and fireworks of joy erupt. This is how I feel when wine and food are perfectly paired to create such an experience.

> *[Humans] don't just survive; they discover; they create...*
> *I mean, just look at what they do with food [and wine]!*
> —Remy

Pairing food and wine has become the focus of many restaurants, wine bars, chefs, and sommeliers. It is the subject of many books. And it's no wonder, because when it is done right, it is so very satisfying. Many people don't have the patience or desire and prefer to eat and drink whatever they like, and that's okay because it is ultimately about the experience, but they are missing out on an expèrience joyeuse, as Remy would say. And of course, on the other end of the spectrum are those diehards on a quest for the perfect combination of fruit, acid, flavor, tannins, and mouthfeel—they are seeking something more like Tchaikovsky's 1812 Overture, cannons and all.

When we owned a wine bar, we featured a local winery every week for what became known as Winemaker Wednesdays. The chef and I would taste through the wines to offer our guests a flight of three three-ounce glasses that would each pair perfectly with tapas style food. We chose the wine first then planned the food to accompany it. As they were all local wines, we chose food that was farmed in the same region, including locally made cheese and olive oil. We were celebrating *farm-to-table* concept, and it was well received. The reason to keep it all local is that the same nutrients and minerals go into everything that's grown in a region. For both food and grapes, exposure to the same weather and topography, the soil, rainfall, temperatures, and sun do have an impact. Sharing these elements brings it all together, the nuances of both the wine and food go hand-in-hand.

While the idea of pairing food and wine in the first century seems like a stretch, it was actually a natural

The Art of Pairing

phenomenon because most of the time the wine from a region was local along with the food. The food and wine from Galilee for example would have elements of the same place, and that speaks to the idea of terroir. So, Jesus would have enjoyed great pairings in His travels regardless of region—whether He realized it or not.

One of my greatest pleasures was planning winemaker dinners—and still is. Knowing my wines intimately, I have zeroed in on what brings out the best in not only the wine, but the food to go with it. While our wines can hold their own, certain pairings make them even more desirable. Adding a splash of the wine I will be pairing to the dish I create provides an expressive sense of harmony.

Wine can be an intimidating subject for some, and rightfully so, because there are over 10,000 different wine grape varietals across many wine-producing countries which have their own wine laws and labeling, with thousands of regions and producers each boasting their unique style. But I stand behind rule number one, drink what you like. I am adventurous and usually like to try something new, so the first thing I do at a restaurant is to peruse the wine menu. If luck would have it, I could speak with the wine captain who would have at least partial sommelier training. If I am buying wine off the shelf in the store, I'll read the back of the label for hints as to what the blend might be, the style, and descriptors of the flavor, and nose (what it smells like). Oftentimes, the label will tell you what food it pairs well with.

Seeking the perfect pairing can be pleasurable and a worthy pursuit. The editors of Wine Enthusiast Magazine say, "It's a sensory and intellectual game that can yield spectacular dividends at the table. Make no mistake: The perfect pairing of wine and food is a sublime experience, elevating both to such an extent that the meal will be blissful at the time, and memorable long after."

Tried and True Pairing Concepts

While there are many possibilities for an interesting pairing, according to Wine Folly, there are some guidelines to help make more consistent choices:

- Consider acidity (which is desired)—the wine should be more acidic than the food.
- Consider sweetness—the wine should be sweeter than the food—this particularly applies to dessert.
- Flavor intensity should be consistent between the wine and food.
- Red wines pair best with bold flavored meats (e.g., red meat).
- White wines pair best with light-intensity meats (e.g., fish or chicken).

The Art of Pairing

- Tannic wines (e.g., red wines) are best balanced with fat.
- It is better to match the wine with the sauce than with the meat.
- More often than not, white, sparkling and Rosé wines create contrasting pairings.
- More often than not, red wines will create congruent pairings.

It's been discovered that there are over twenty different tastes found in food, but when pairing food and wine you only need to focus on six main tastes: Salt, Acid, Sweet, Bitter, Fat, and Spice. Determining which of these dominates will help you mimic the taste. An easy and natural way to combine food and wine is to mirror what you pair. This means you pair two similar characteristics to bring out the best in that attribute. Some natural mirrored combinations are lobster with a buttery Chardonnay, or a peppery stir fry with a peppery Syrah. And as I mentioned, if you add a splash of the wine you will be pairing as an ingredient to the dish you are making, the flavors will be anchored.

> *"I haven't had much luck with pairing red wine with lobster."* —Michael Broadbent

What Would Jesus Pair?

Digging deeper, the next thing to consider is the power and weight of both the food and the wine. You've just ordered a dish of delicate scallops; what happens when you have it with a bold Cabernet? All you would taste is the bold wine. Conversely, if you were to serve boeuf bourguignon (a hearty beef stew made with Burgundy wine) with a lovely Chenin Blanc from the Loire region in France, all you would taste is the stew, because it would completely overpower the delicate wine. These two scenarios do injustice to both the food and the wine. A good basic rule to follow is this: heavy dishes with heavy wines, robust dishes with robust wines, light dishes with light wines, and delicate dishes with delicate wine. There are a number of charts available to help determine which wines pair with certain foods.

Another technique is to juxtapose the flavors of the food and wine. You can round out a spicy dish with off-dry aromatic white wines without compromising the excitement the spice brings to the food. I particularly like a dry Riesling, a not-so-sweet Gewürztraminer, or especially a viscous Viognier (an amazing wine Rhône) with spicy food to create a beautiful balance.

Matching fat to the dish's profile is also important. When you determine the amount and type (animal- or vegetable-based) of fat in a dish, think about the acidity or tannin in the wine. For example, a high-acid white wine such as Sauvignon Blanc pairs well with an acid-based fat

The Art of Pairing

like a lemon-butter sauce, fresh goat cheese or avocado-lime salsa. A tannic red wine such as a Merlot or Cabernet Sauvignon will do better with a protein-based fat: butter, cream or a thickened broth-based sauce like a demi-glace.

Contrary to belief, you can drink red with fish. Can you pair a flaky white fish with a big, full-bodied Cabernet Sauvignon? Sure, you can! But try balancing the lighter weight of the fish with an umami-heavy ingredient such as sautéed mushrooms. And because the tannins in Cabernet Sauvignon cry out for fat, add a red wine-based beurre blanc—and don't forget the salt. Or why not try a grilled flank steak with Sauvignon Blanc? The weight of the meat is heavy for the wine so lighten it up by turning it into tacos. Add a cabbage coleslaw as a counterpoint to the weight of the meat and garnish with an acid-based fat like guacamole.

Dessert pairings can elude me for some reason, perhaps it's because I don't usually have a sweet tooth, and also by the time I have finished a meal I am satiated enough to forgo this last course. Truth be told, I have had some not-so-pleasant dessert pairings. But all is not lost. Sweetness is the main thing to consider for the last and final course. Sweetness in the food will make the wine taste drier and that's not a good pairing for dessert. A luscious piece of chocolate cake will be complemented by nicely chilled dessert wine such as Madeira, Port, Muscat, or sweet Riesling, and will bring a good balance of sweetness and acidity. There's plenty of fat in cheesecake, so a sweet Riesling, or Sauvignon Blanc holds its own even if it is topped with a fruit sauce or compote. While it's customary to begin a celebratory event with a glass of Champagne or Prosecco, if you are serving fresh fruit—especially chocolate-dipped strawberries—this is a lovely accompaniment. This combo also makes for a light dessert.

Cheese and wine are at the top of my list of things to start or end a meal. The custom of serving cheese for dessert in France is one that we have adopted for ourselves. They are a natural combination, and a little knowledge goes a long way. Both the cheese and the wine should have the same intensity. A delicate Gruyère would do nicely with a lighter Pinot Noir. Alcohol matters, if you have a wine over 14.5 percent (which a lot of California reds boast), then you want a more intense cheese. Italian reds are pretty intense and stand up to Italian cheese like Asiago, Pecorino-Romano, or Provolone to name a few.

Wine that has 12 percent or less alcohol requires delicately flavored cheese, a Triple-Creme Brie or Camembert would match well with Pinot Grigio, Viognier, or Chenin Blanc. Chardonnay can get pretty oaky or buttery and can stand up to the big flavors of an aged cheddar, aged gouda, or even parmesan. And my favorite—soft cheeses like brie, camembert, and goat cheese are great with champagne. Their creamy texture and mild flavor balance well with the acidity of the wine.

Finally, if I am enjoying an Italian meal, then I automatically have Italian wine—and my favorite duo is Chianti with pizza; the same holds true for French, German, and Spanish cuisine, and all major wine regions of the world. Keeping in mind the simple guidelines I provided, the wine and food from the same respective region will produce an overall pleasurable experience.

There is a whole world of food and wine pairing to explore that won't fit into one chapter, so if you are inclined you might just find a new passion in the art of pairing. Be fearless, be creative, and enjoy. Good food and wine are proof that God loves us.

And finally, this brings us to the main question. What would Jesus pair?

I believe Jesus had a discerning palate. He knew that the food He was eating and the wine He was drinking was a gift from His Father and meant to nourish both body and soul beyond mere sustenance. Wine was the prevalent beverage of the times, and He would have experienced a wide variety depending upon where He was and who was serving it. When Jesus dined with the Pharisees, or the wealthier of society, the wine would have been of a higher quality and likely from Pompeii, ancient Rome's highly prized wine center. The best wine came from Greece and that included a variety of really great white wines.

What Would Jesus Pair?

In general, the wine Jesus drank in His travels would have been very robust and would not have been well aged. Those wines were cut with water (often seawater), and enhanced with honey, herbs, spices, or other organic substances like resin. They would not have been like the yummy wines we have come to enjoy today. While there is a lot of speculation, it is believed that the wine at the Last Supper was very much like a modern Italian Amarone, although not as refined or complex. It was made with grapes that were dried after harvest, giving it a unique, big flavor with a lot of tannins because of the grape skins. Amarone translates to "big-bitter." This would have paired well with the gamey lamb stew at that last Passover meal.

I often wonder what wine Jesus provided when He cooked fish over a fire on the beach as He waited for the disciples. What about the wine He shared with Mary, Martha, and Lazarus? Matthew was a tax collector before He was called by Jesus to follow Him, so chances are the wine he served to Jesus and his friends was likely a little higher quality and from Pompeii. As Jesus and the disciples traveled, they would have been guests of those they met along the way and the wine would have varied depending on the circumstances and locale of the host.

If you travel to Israel today and visit Cana, you may be able to purchase "Cana wine." It is thick, sweet, and deep red. The sweetness may be a lot for some palates,

The Art of Pairing

and you might understand why some Jews of Jesus' day had adopted the Greek habit of cutting wine with water. More than having a heavy sweetness, though, a lot of wine in Jesus' day was not very good. Adding water made it more palatable. This was especially true as the year went on and older wine would spoil or turn vinegary.

—Patricia Kasten

The water Jesus turned into wine at the wedding at Cana would have been the best of the best, after all it was a heavenly vintage. It is no coincidence that transforming water into wine was His first public miracle; and Jesus' final gesture when He offered up a chalice of wine to drink in remembrance—to symbolize His blood that would be shed to save you and me.

Good wine and food are proof that God loves us.

Happy pairing.

23

The Recipes

BREADS AND BREAKFAST

Solomon's Flat Bread (Crackers)
(When baked a little longer, this makes a great cracker for Mediterranean dips like tapenade and hummus).

INGREDIENTS
    1 1/2 cups whole wheat flour
    1/3 cup fine cornmeal
    1 tbsp olive oil
    1 1/2 tsp salt
    1/2 cup cooked lentils
    1 tbsp millet, ground into powder
    1 1/2 cups water
    1 tsp onion powder
    1/2 cup sesame seeds

Preheat the oven to 350 degrees F. Combine flour, cornmeal, olive oil, salt, lentils, millet, and water to make a dough mixture and flatten onto an oiled baking sheet.

Sprinkle the top with onion powder and sesame seeds. Bake for 20 minutes or so. For a crispier cracker, leave in the oven for an additional 10 minutes. Makes 6 servings.

Wine Pairing: Choose a wine that will pair with the main dish/dip it will accompany (e.g., Mediterranean tapenade and hummus: Dry white [Viognier, Pinot Grigio, Pinot Blanc, Chenin Blanc] or Dry Rosé)

(*Cooking with the Bible* by Anthony Chiffolo and Rayner Hesse, Jr., copyright 2009, page 96)

Ezekiel's Bread

"And you, take wheat and barley, beans and lentils, millet and emmer, and put them into a single vessel and make your bread from them." —Ezekiel 4:9

God commanded Ezekiel to bake this bread as part of His message to the people of Jerusalem.

INGREDIENTS
- 1 tbsp plus 2 tsp active dry yeast
- 1 1/2 cups warm water (105 - 110 degrees F)
- 3 cups white bread flour
- 1 3/4 cups stone ground spelt flour
- 1/2 cup barley flour
- 1/4 cup dry lentils, finely ground

1/4 cup dry fava beans, finely ground
1 tbsp millet
1 tbsp salt
1/4 cup plus 2 tbsp olive oil
3 tbsp bee or date honey
1/2 cup barley grits
1 tbsp coriander seeds, coarsely crushed

In a small bowl, dissolve yeast in 1/4 cup warm water. Let stand until it starts to bubble, 10 to 15 minutes.

In a large mixing bowl, combine white flour, spelt flour, barley grits, ground lentils, ground faves, millet and salt. Stir to blend. Make a well in the center and add yeast mixture, 1/4 cup olive oil, and honey. Mix thoroughly, adding remaining water (2 Tbsp) at a time until loose dough forms. Transfer to a floured work surface and knead until dough becomes soft and elastic, 10 to 12 minutes. Shape into a large ball. Cover with a kitchen towel and let rest for 3 to 4 minutes, then knead vigorously for one more minute.

Lightly grease two baking sheets and sprinkle generously with barley grits. Divide dough into two equal portions. Form into eight-inch rounds. Set on a baking sheet and cover with a kitchen towel. Set aside in a warm, draft free area (75 - 80 degrees F) and let rise until they double in size.

Preheat the oven to 400 degrees F. Coat each round with olive oil. Sprinkle the loaves with coriander seeds. Bake until crusty and brown and the underside sounds hollow when tapped, 40 to 45 minutes. Makes two 10-inch loaves.

Wine Pairing: Choose a wine that will pair with the protein course, or the main dish this will accompany.

(*A Biblical Feast written by Kitty Morse*, Copyright 2009, published by La Caravane, Vista California)

Easy Flatbread (No Yeast)

INGREDIENTS

    2 cups all-purpose flour
    1 1/2 tsp baking powder
    1 tsp fine sea salt
    2 tbsp olive oil
    1 tsp pure maple syrup or sugar
    3/4 cup cold water
    Vegetable oil for cooking

Make the dough: in a large bowl, whisk the flour, baking powder, and salt together until well blended. Make a well in the middle of the flour mixture, and then add olive oil, maple syrup, and most of the water (saving a few tablespoons to add later as necessary). Switch to a rubber spatula or spoon and stir the wet ingredients into the flour mixture. If the dough seems dry, add the remaining water. When the dough comes together, transfer to a floured work surface and knead 5 to 10 times until smooth. Cover with a clean dish cloth and leave for 10 minutes.

Cook the flatbreads: divide the dough into six equal pieces. Dust each piece in flour and roll into a disc that's between 1/8-inch and 1/4-inch thick. (Rolling thinner will make thinner bread that's less soft in the middle. Rolling thicker will make thicker, fluffier bread.)

Add 1 to 2 tbsp of oil to a skillet placed over medium heat. When the oil looks shimmery, add a flatbread (or more if they fit), and cook until golden brown on one side, flip and cook until golden brown on the second side, 1 to 2 minutes on each side.

Transfer cooked flatbread to a plate, cover with a clean dish towel to keep warm, and then continue with the remaining flatbread. If the skillet looks dry, add a little more oil before continuing. Makes six.

Wine Pairing: Choose a wine that will pair with the main dish it will accompany (e.g., Mediterranean tapenade and hummus: Dry White [Viognier, Pinot Grigio, Pinot Blanc, Chenin Blanc] or Dry Rosé)

(InspiredTaste.com, recipe by Adam and Joanne Gallagher)

Biblical Barley Cakes (Biscuits)

INGREDIENTS
  1 1/2 cup barley flour
  1/2 cup whole wheat flour
  1 tsp baking powder
  1/2 tsp salt
  1 cup whole milk
  1 egg
  1 cup honey

Preheat the oven to 425 degrees F. In a medium bowl combine barley flour, whole wheat flour, baking powder, and salt. In a separate medium bowl, whisk together the milk, egg, and honey. Stir the dry ingredients into the wet ingredients until blended.

Grease a muffin tin with oil. Drop the mixture by the spoonful into the prepared muffin tin. Bake for 10-15 minutes. Cakes will be light brown when done. Makes twelve mini-cakes.

Wine Pairing: Choose a wine that will pair with the main dish it will accompany.

(Inspired by: The BiblicalNutritionist.com, recipe by Annette Reeder)

Creamy Barley Breakfast Porridge

INGREDIENTS
- 1 tbsp unsalted butter
- 1 cup pearl barley
- Pinch of fine salt
- 1 tsp ground cinnamon
- 3 cups water
- 1 cup milk nut, oat, or regular milk
- 1/2 tsp vanilla extract
- 3-4 tbsp packed light brown sugar

Melt the butter in a saucepan over medium heat. Add the pearl barley and cook, stirring frequently, until the barley grains are toasty and fragrant, about 3 minutes.

Add the salt, cinnamon, water, milk and vanilla extract and bring to a boil. Stir briefly and turn the heat down to low. Cover and simmer, stirring occasionally, until barley is creamy and tender, about 40 minutes. Add additional water as necessary if the porridge becomes too thick or sticks to the bottom of the saucepan.

Remove from the heat, add the brown sugar and stir to combine. Add additional sugar and/or salt to taste and adjust the consistency as necessary with another splash or two of water. Serve topped with additional milk, cream, or other toppings of choice.

What Would Jesus Pair?

Suggested Toppings:

Sliced fresh fruit and/or berries
Dried fruit such as dates, figs, or apricots
Fruit compote
Toasted or roasted nuts
Honey or maple syrup

Serves four.

(True-North-Kitchen.com, recipe by Kristi Bissell)

APPETIZERS / CHARCUTERIE

Spiced Wine

INGREDIENTS

    1 (750 ml.) bottle red wine (not expensive—bolder wine is better)
    2 oranges (blood oranges are best when in season)
    6 whole cloves
    3 cinnamon sticks, plus more for garnish
    4 star anise
    1 2-inch piece fresh ginger, peeled and sliced
    4 green cardamom seeds (optional)
    1/4 cup honey
    1/2 cup brandy

Remove the peel of 1 orange in strips then juice it. Slice the other orange into rounds and save for garnish.

In a large pot or saucepan, combine the orange peel and juice along with the remainder of the ingredients. Stir over medium heat to combine. Bring the wine to a low boil then immediately reduce the heat to low. Simmer gently, for at least 30 minutes.

Ladle into cups or mugs. Garnish each with an orange slice and cinnamon sticks (optional). Serves four to six.

Classic Marinated Olives

INGREDIENTS
    Total of: 16 oz jarred pitted olives, such as jumbo Kalamata and Castelvetrano olives, drained & rinsed
    4 cloves garlic, thinly sliced
    2 sprigs rosemary
    8–10 sprigs thyme
    1 bay leaf
    lemon rind from 1/2 lemon
    optional: 1 teaspoon crushed red chili flakes
    1 cup olive oil

Layer all ingredients except the olive oil in a 16 oz glass jar. Slowly pour in the olive oil making sure everything is exposed to the oil. Close the jar tightly and let the olives marinate in the refrigerator for a minimum of two days up to seven days (they will keep up to 3 months). Serve at room temperature with your favorite charcuterie. Makes one pound.

Wine Pairing: Olives pair with a wide range of wine, so I suggest you pair them with the cheese or other items that accompany them.

The Recipes

Olive Tapenade

INGREDIENTS

    2 cups mixed pitted olives drained (such as black, Kalamata, and ripe green)
    4 tbsp fresh flat-leaf parsley, chopped
    1 tbsp fresh basil leaves, chopped
    2 tbsp marinated sun-dried tomatoes, drained and chopped
    1/4 cup extra virgin olive oil
    3-4 medium cloves garlic, pressed or minced
    1 tbsp lemon juice
    Fresh ground black pepper to taste

Add all ingredients to the bowl of a food processor and pulse 15-20 times for a chunky dip (scraping down the bowl in between). For a spread, process until desired texture. Transfer to a serving bowl and enjoy with your favorite crostini, pita, crackers, cheese, or on a charcuterie, and especially with hummus. Serves six.

Wine Pairing: Dry White (Viognier, Pinot Grigio, Pinot Blanc, Chenin Blanc), or Rosé (Provence), or Vouvray (Loire Valley), or Sparkling White.

Hummus

INGREDIENTS

    1 -15 oz can garbanzo beans (chickpeas), drained and rinsed
    2 to 4 tbsps water
    2 tbsp extra virgin olive oil
    1 tbsp fresh lemon juice
    1 garlic clove, minced
    1/4 cup tahini
    1/4 - 1/2 tsp salt (use larger amount if not using cumin)
    Optional fresh herbs: up to 1/2 cup cilantro, basil, or parsley (or a combo of all three), and/or 3/4 tsp smoked or sweet paprika, cumin, or any Mediterranean spice blend of your choice.

Add all ingredients to the bowl of a food processor and blend until smooth and creamy. Add more water to thin out hummus while blending if necessary for a better texture. Serves six. (Inspired by my friend, Chelsey Hasenohr)

Wine Pairing: Dry White (Viognier, Pinot Grigio, Pinot Blanc, Chenin Blanc) or Dry Rosé.

Dolmas (Stuffed Grape Leaves)

INGREDIENTS
- 1 16 oz jar grape leaves
- 2 cups uncooked long-grain white rice
- 1 large sweet onion, chopped
- 1/2 cup chopped fresh dill
- 1/2 cup chopped fresh mint leaves
- 1/2 cup pine nuts
- 2 quarts chicken broth, divided
- 3/4 cup fresh lemon juice, divided
- 1 cup olive oil, divided

Carefully remove the grape leaves from the jar and rinse very well under cold water. Bring a pot of water to a boil, and blanch the leaves, in batches, for 4-5 minutes. Remove to a colander and rinse with cold water and set aside.

In a large saucepan over medium-high heat sauté 1/2 cup olive oil, uncooked rice, onion, dill, mint, and pine nuts until onions are translucent—about 5 minutes. Add 4 cups of the broth and reduce the heat to low, and simmer until rice is cooked through approx. 15 minutes. Stir in 1/2 of the lemon juice, remove from the heat and set aside.

Place a grape leaf onto a work surface with the shiny side facing down. The underside of the leaf should be face up (the veins of the leaf are on this side). Using the point of a sharp paring knife, cut out the stem of the leaf. Place 1 tbsp of rice mixture on the bottom center of the leaf, just above the stem. Fold the bottom up just over the filling, then both sides in toward the center and roll up from the bottom to the top. Place rolled bundles into a 4-quart pot with the seam down, packing them into the pot tightly so they don't open while cooking.

Pour remaining 1/2 cup olive oil and remaining lemon juice over leaves, then pour in remaining 4 cups of broth to cover. Place an inverted heatproof plate on top of the rolls to keep them submerged in the water. Cover the pot and simmer for approx. 45 minutes to 1 hour. Note: Do not let it boil as the filling may burst out of the leaves.

Gently remove onto a platter and let cool for 30 minutes. They may be served at room temperature or chilled. Either way, serve with slices of fresh lemons. Makes approx. sixty dolmas.

Wine Pairing: Aromatic White wines from Greece, or Albariño (Spain), or Vermentino (Italy), or Sauvignon Blanc.

Grape and Prosciutto Crostini

INGREDIENTS
- 1 baguette, cut into 1/4 -inch slices
- 4 tbsp olive oil
- 36 green, red, and/or black seedless grapes
- 1 tbsp balsamic vinegar
- 1/2 tbsp honey
- Freshly ground pepper to taste
- 4 oz. soft goat cheese
- 6 slices prosciutto
- 1/2 cup baby arugula (or preferred microgreens)

Preheat the oven to 350 degrees F. Lightly brush 12 slices of baguette with half of the olive oil and lay them directly on the middle rack of the oven. Toast for 5 minutes, or until light golden brown. Let cool to room temperature and arrange on a serving platter or board.

To make the dressing, whisk together the vinegar, olive oil, honey, salt and pepper, set aside.

Place a half slice of prosciutto on each crostini. Top with a little goat cheese, a few baby arugula leaves, and 6 grape halves.

Drizzle dressing over the crostini and serve immediately. Makes twelve Crostini Appetizers.

Wine Pairing: Napa Valley Fumé Blanc, Chenin Blanc, Viognier, or Sparkling Rosé.

Spiced Pear and Pomegranate Crostini

INGREDIENTS

    Baguette, sliced into 1/2-inch thickness (6 slices)
    Olive oil
    2 large ripe, firm pears, peeled and diced
    2 tbsp butter
    1/2 tsp cinnamon
    1/8 tsp nutmeg
    1/8 tsp ginger
    1/4 cup quality maple syrup
    1 tsp aged balsamic vinegar
    1 cup Pomegranate seeds (arils)
    1/2 walnut pieces (optional)
    1 - 6 oz package cinnamon cream cheese

Preheat the oven to 350 degrees F. Lightly brush the baguette slices with olive oil and lay them directly on the middle rack of the oven. Toast for 5 minutes, or until light golden brown. Let cool to room temperature. Generously spread each slice with cinnamon cream cheese and arrange on a serving platter or board. Set aside.

Melt the butter in a pan over medium heat. Add the diced pears, cinnamon, nutmeg, ginger, and maple syrup and sauté for 3-5 minutes until warmed through. Remove from heat and stir in the balsamic vinegar, pomegranate arils, and walnuts (if using). Using a slotted spoon, top each crostini with the warm fruit mixture and then drizzle the tops with a small amount of the remaining fruit syrup. Serve immediately.

Variation: Use 4 oz of goat cheese in place of cream cheese for an interesting balance. Serves six.

Wine Pairing: Sweeter Vouvray (Chenin Blanc Gold), Riesling that is medium-dry, or sweet white wines from Bordeaux (Sauternes and Barsac—that is if you have expensive taste). *If you use goat cheese instead of cream cheese, consider: Vouvray (not sweet), Chenin Blanc, or Sauvignon Blanc.

Brie en Croûte with Thyme and Fig Jam

INGREDIENTS

    1 - 6 to 8 oz round triple crème brie, or camembert for more intense flavor, slightly chilled

    10-inch square chilled puff pastry dough

    All-purpose flour, for dusting

    Fig jam

    1/2 tsp fresh thyme leaves (from 2 medium stems), plus 3 - 4 stems for garnish

    1 large egg beaten with 1 Tbsp water

Preheat the oven to 350 degrees F. Using a sharp knife, carefully cut off the top rind of the cheese and discard. Slightly score the top of the cheese.

Roll puff pastry on a lightly floured surface to 1/4-inch thickness. Place cheese in the center of the pastry and spread a few tablespoons of fig jam evenly and top with thyme leaves. Fold dough up and over sides of cheese, pleating it on top to encase the cheese. Brush some of the egg wash between the pleats to help seal the pastry. Reserve the rest of the egg wash for baking. Wrap in plastic wrap and chill for at least 20 minutes.

Place the pastry encased cheese wheel on a parchment lined baking sheet and brush evenly with remaining egg wash. Bake until pastry is golden brown, 25 to 35 minutes. Let rest for 5 minutes, then serve garnished with a few sprigs of thyme.

Serving suggestion: water crackers, apples, pears, grapes, and almonds.

Wine Pairing: Viognier (or White Rhône blend), Alsatian Riesling, or a Dry White Sparkling.

Goat Cheese Stuffed Dates

INGREDIENTS

    20 large Medjool dates

    4 ounces goat cheese, room temperature

    1/3 cup walnut pieces

    Warmed honey, for garnish

    Red pepper flakes or Aleppo pepper (optional)

Preheat the oven to 350 degrees F. Slice the dates lengthwise on one side to create an opening and remove the pit (if not already pitted).

Using a small spoon, fill the date with goat cheese, and gently push walnuts into the goat cheese. Place them on a large sheet pan lined with parchment. Bake for 5 to 10 minutes, or until the dates have softened and warmed through. Remove from the oven and finish with a drizzle of honey and pepper flakes. Transfer to a serving plate or board and serve immediately.

Variations:

Spanish Style:

    Stuff with Manchego Cheese, and Marcona Almonds (drizzled with honey).

Bacon Wrapped:

Wrap each stuffed date 1 and 1/2 times with a slice of thin bacon. Secure with a toothpick. Bake for 10 minutes, remove from the oven and using a toothpick turn each one on its side and return to the oven for additional 5-8 minutes—or until bacon is done to your liking.

Wine Pairing: Chardonnay, Dry Rosé, White or Rosé Sparkling.

Pomegranate Relish

(Serve on crostini with Manchego (sheep's cheese) or Brie)

INGREDIENTS

1/2 cup Pomegranate arils
1 tbsp pomegranate molasses (see recipe)
3 tbsp finely diced shallots
1 tsp lemon juice
1/4 cup extra virgin olive oil
1 tbsp chopped flat-leaf parsley or fresh chopped mint
Salt and freshly ground black pepper to taste

For Pomegranate Molasses:
3 cups 100 percent pomegranate juice
1/4 cup sugar
1 lemon, juiced

Combine all pomegranate molasses ingredients in a saucepan, bring to a simmer and reduce until a very thick syrup forms. Cool to room temperature.

Place the shallots, lemon juice, and 1/4 tsp salt in a small bowl and let sit for 5 minutes. Whisk in the pomegranate molasses and then the olive oil. Stir in the fresh pomegranate arils and the parsley or mint. Season with salt and pepper to taste. Serves four.

Wine Pairing: Sparkling Rosé, Italian Prosecco, Riesling, or Pinot Noir.

Gefilte Fish Appetizer (Doctored from a jar)

INGREDIENTS
    2 -24 ounce jars gefilte fish (any store bought brand)
    Extra virgin olive oil
    4 carrots, sliced crosswise
    1 large onion, sliced thin
    4 celery ribs, cut into small pieces
    Ground black pepper

Place very little olive oil in a pot over medium heat. Add the onion and just slightly brown. Add the pieces of fish and the fish gelatin, carrots, celery and pepper to taste. Raise the flame to high and bring to a boil and then reduce the heat back to medium or medium-low and simmer for 8 to 10 minutes. Remove from heat.

Take the pieces of fish out of the pot very gently and cool on a platter. Reserve the vegetables. Slightly oil a cookie sheet. Lay the pieces of fish onto the slightly oiled cookie sheet and turn the fish over, so that both sides of the fish are oiled. Place the fish into a preheated 350 degree F oven for 10 minutes. Turn the fish over and bake for another 10 minutes, or until the fish is slightly browned. Remove from the oven and refrigerate. Serve with the reserved vegetables and horseradish. Serves six.

Wine Pairing: Chenin Blanc, German Riesling, Sauvignon Blanc. (food.com, recipe submitted by Alan Leonetti)

The Recipes

SOUPS

Mimi's Lentil Soup

INGREDIENTS
- 2 tbsp olive oil
- 1 medium onion, chopped (white or yellow)
- 3 garlic cloves, minced
- 1 large carrot chopped (about 1 1/4 cups)
- 2 celery ribs chopped (about 1 1/4 cups)
- 8 baby potatoes
- 2 cups dried lentils, green, or brown, rinsed (red are also an option * see note)
- 1 -14 oz can crushed tomatoes
- 1 1/2 quarts (6 cups) vegetable or chicken stock / broth, low sodium
- 1 tsp each cumin and coriander powder
- 1 1/2 tsp paprika powder (smoked paprika gives it a nice warm flavor and aroma)
- 1/2 tsp each salt and black pepper (or more to taste)
- 3 cups baby spinach

Heat oil in a large pot over medium heat. Add onion and cook for 2 minutes. Add celery, carrot, and garlic. Cook for 7-10 minutes or until softened, being careful not to brown the garlic. Add all remaining ingredients except spinach and increase to high heat until it begins to boil. Immediately reduce to medium heat and let simmer. Scoop scum on the surface off and discard during cooking if required. Place lid on and cook for 35-40 minutes or until lentils are soft. *NOTE: red lentils will cook faster between 15-20 minutes. Add the baby spinach at the very end before serving so it retains its bright color.

For a thicker soup you can use an immersion blender to blend some of the lentils before adding the spinach. The red lentils will be thicker and creamier on their own.

Add a touch of water if you want to adjust soup consistency. Season to taste with salt and pepper. You can heat things up by adding cayenne pepper to taste. Serves six.

Wine Pairing: Dry White, such as Viognier or Côtes de Provence (from Rhône Valley, or Provence), or a Red: Pinot Noir, Chianti Classico. *As my mother hails from Germany and we grew up on German wines, our family would enjoy this soup with a German wine from the Mosel region.

Inspired by my mother, Wilhelmine (Mimi) Hill

Classic Chicken Matzah Ball Soup

INGREDIENTS

For the Soup (make 1 day ahead if desired):
1 (4 to 5) pound chicken whole or cut into pieces
3 medium yellow onions, leaving the skin on and quartered
6 carrots, peeled and roughly chopped
5 celery stalks with greens, roughly chopped
2 bay leaves
About 10 fresh parsley sprigs
1/4 tsp celery seed
Salt, to taste
White pepper, to taste
About 2 tbsp chicken bouillon powder

For Matzah Balls:
1 box Streit's or Manischewitz Matzo* Ball Mix (2 bags of matzo ball mix)
Additional 5 quarts chicken broth/stock or water (do not use the soup base you made above)

*Matzah is spelled different ways, so the package will say matzo

For Serving:
4 carrots, peeled and cut into 1-inch pieces
4 stalks celery washed and cut into 1-inch pieces
1/4 cup freshly chopped parsley, dill, or chives

In a large stock pot filled with 6 quarts of water, add the washed chicken (without giblets), onions (with root end removed), carrots, and celery and bring to a boil. Let the soup simmer, uncovered, for 30 minutes. Be sure to skim off any froth or scum from the top. Reduce the flame to low and add the bay leaves, parsley, celery seed, 2 tsp of salt, and 1/4 tsp white pepper. Cover and simmer for 3-4 hours. Let the soup cool for 20-30 minutes. Remove the chicken and pull meat off the bone and shred—set aside. Place a fine mesh strainer over a very large soup pot and pour the soup through the strainer to strain out all the remaining solids. Refrigerate the soup stock overnight if desired.

Skim most (but not all) of the fat from the surface of the soup and discard. A little bit of fat in the soup adds flavor, so add some back in from the strainer if need be. Add the bouillon, salt (approx. 2 tsp), and white pepper (approx. 1/4 tsp) and bring to a gentle simmer while making the matzah balls according to the package directions and boil in a separate pot of water (or broth/stock). Don't make the matzah balls in the chicken stock you made because they will soak up much of the good soup.

With a slotted spoon, add the cooked (boiled) matzah balls to the simmering pot of soup as well as the carrots and celery. Continue to simmer for 20-30 minutes. Fluffy matzah balls should rise to the top when they are ready. Add the shredded chicken and chopped parsley, dill, or chives. Simmer for a few more minutes. Ladle into bowls and enjoy this dose of comfort. Serves ten to twelve.

Wine Pairing: White Sparkling, Viognier, Grenache Blanc, Soft Chardonnay (not oaky).

SALADS AND SIDES

Vanilla Fig Dressing

(Great for dressing salads with pears, walnuts, and arugula)

1/3 cup light olive oil
1/3 cup aged balsamic vinegar
1/3 cup prepared fig jam
1 tsp vanilla
1 tsp each salt and pepper

Whisk together all ingredients until blended or shake until blended in a glass jar. Store in the refrigerator. Makes approx. one cup.

Egyptian Barley Salad with Pomegranate Vinaigrette

INGREDIENTS

1 1/2 cups pearl barley (do not substitute hulled barley or hull-less barley)
Salt and pepper
1/4 cup extra virgin olive oil, plus more for serving
2 1/2 tbsp pomegranate molasses (see recipe below)
1 tsp fresh lemon juice
1 tbsp sugar

1/2 tsp ground cinnamon

1/2 tsp ground cumin

1/2 cup coarsely chopped fresh cilantro (parsley may be substituted)

1/2 cup golden raisins

1/2 cup unsalted shelled pistachios or walnuts, chopped coarse

4 oz feta cheese, cut into 1/2-inch cubes

1/2 cup scallions, green parts only, thinly sliced (you'll need 4 to 6 scallions)

1/2 cup pomegranate seeds (arils)

For Pomegranate Molasses:
3 cups 100 percent pomegranate juice

1/4 cup sugar

1 lemon, juiced

Combine all pomegranate molasses ingredients in a saucepan, bring to a simmer and reduce until a very thick syrup forms. Cool to room temperature.

Bring 4 quarts of water to boil in a large pot or Dutch oven. Add barley and 1 tbsp salt, return to boil, and cook until tender, about 45 minutes, or according to package instructions. Drain the barley, spread onto a rimmed baking sheet, and let cool completely, about 15 minutes.

In a large bowl, whisk together the oil, pomegranate molasses, lemon juice, sugar, cinnamon, cumin, and 1/4 tsp salt. Add the barley, cilantro, raisins, and pistachios (or walnuts) and gently toss to combine. Season with salt and pepper to taste. Spread barley salad evenly on a serving platter and arrange feta, scallions, and pomegranate seeds in separate diagonal rows on top. Drizzle with extra oil and serve.

Make Ahead: the cooked barley and vinaigrette can be refrigerated separately for up to 3 days. To serve, bring barley and vinaigrette to room temperature, whisk vinaigrette to recombine, and continue with step 3, seasoning to taste as necessary. Dressed salad can be held up to 2 hours at room temperature before serving. Serves six to eight.

Wine Pairing: Sparkling Rosé, Viognier, Dry Riesling.

(OnceUponaChef.com, recipe by Jenn Segal)

Classic Mediterranean Tabbouleh Salad

(Tabouli is a Middle Eastern vegetarian salad that is made up mostly of fresh-chopped parsley and seasoned with olive oil, lemon juice, and salt).

INGREDIENTS

1 1/2 cup fine bulgur wheat

1 cup boiling water

4 firm Roma tomatoes, finely diced

1 English cucumber (do not remove skin), finely chopped

4 scallions, finely sliced

3 big bunches of parsley (not cilantro), washed and finely chopped in a food processor

3/4 cup freshly squeezed lemon or lime juice

1/3 cup olive oil

1/2 tsp salt or to taste

12 fresh mint leaves, finely chopped (optional)

Rinse bulgur wheat in a fine mesh strainer. In a medium bowl, combine the bulgur and 1 cup of boiling water. Cover it with a plate and let it soak for at least 15 minutes, or until all the water is absorbed. Test to see that it is tender, if not add a bit more boiling water and let rest until water is absorbed. Return to the fine mesh strainer and press out any excess water. Set aside.

Drain chopped tomatoes in a colander. In a medium bowl, add the tomatoes, cucumbers, and scallions. Mix in the parsley (preferably chopped in a food processor) and finely chopped mint leaves. Gently fold in the drained bulgur and season with salt to taste. Now add the lemon or lime juice and olive oil and gently mix again. Refrigerate covered for at least 30 minutes or until ready to serve. Serves six to eight.

Wine Pairing: Sauvignon Blanc, Riesling, or Gruner Veltliner.

What Would Jesus Pair?

Roasted Beet Salad with Lentils and Goat Cheese

INGREDIENTS

Dressing:
1/2 cup pomegranate juice
2 tbsp shallot, chopped fine
2 tbsp red wine vinegar or champagne vinegar
4 tbsp olive oil
2 tbsp honey
1 tbsp orange zest, finely chopped
1/2 tsp each salt and black pepper
1 lb. red baby beets, tops removed
10 oz dry green lentils
5 oz goat cheese crumbles or feta crumbles
1 small red onion, peeled and finely sliced
1 cup baby arugula

Preheat the oven to 400 degrees F. Wash the beets thoroughly. With a sharp knife slice off approx. 1/4 inch of the bottom and top of the beets. Place them evenly spaced in a round, metal baking tin and pour water around them to reach about 1/3 up the beets. Drizzle with olive oil and add a few sprigs of fresh herbs (parsley and thyme are my favorite). Cover with aluminum foil and roast in the oven for 50—60 minutes until cooked through and tender. Remove to a work surface and let cool to the touch. The peels should easily slide off, if not gently peel them with a sharp paring knife. Cut into bite sized pieces.

Meanwhile, place the lentils in a small cooking pot and fill up with water, place over a high heat and bring to a boil. Reduce the heat and simmer for 20 minutes until tender. Drain and rinse under cold water and place in a medium or large bowl.

Whisk together all dressing ingredients or shake in a jar until blended. Add the dressing to the bowl of lentils to coat them. Then add to the bowl the roasted beets, goat cheese or feta crumbles, red onion and baby arugula and toss to combine. Serve immediately on a large serving platter. Serves six.

Wine Pairing: Dry Sparking, medium bodied Viognier, Dry Rosé, or Pinot Noir.

Brown Butter Lentil and Sweet Potato Salad

INGREDIENTS

    1 pound sweet potatoes, or butternut squash and cut into 3/4 inch pieces (about 4 cups)
    2 tbsp olive oil
    Kosher salt and black pepper
    1 cup French green lentils or black lentils, rinsed
    1/2 cup chopped fresh parsley leaves and tender stems
    1/2 cup crumbled goat cheese (optional)

    Brown Butter Vinaigrette:
    1 tbsp minced fresh sage leaves
    4 tbsp unsalted butter
    1 tbsp extra-virgin olive oil
    2 tbsp red wine vinegar
    1 tsp maple syrup (or honey)
    Kosher salt and black pepper

Preheat the oven to 375 degrees F. and set a rack in the center. Prepare the sweet potatoes: On a baking sheet, toss the sweet potatoes with the olive oil and a sprinkle of salt and pepper. Spread into an even layer and roast, stirring occasionally, until golden and tender, 15 to 25 minutes. While the sweet potatoes cook, prepare the lentils: Add the lentils to a medium pot and cover with about 6 cups of water. Salt the water generously and bring the mixture to a boil. Turn the heat down to a simmer and cook the lentils until just tender, 15 to 25 minutes. Drain the lentils then return them to the pot. Cover to keep warm. Prepare the vinaigrette: Add the sage to a small bowl. Melt the butter in a small skillet set over medium heat (use a pan with a light interior so you can easily see the milk solids change color). Cook the butter for a few minutes, stirring occasionally and scraping the milk solids off the bottom and sides of the pan as needed, until the milk solids turn golden brown and smell toasty. Pour the hot browned butter and all of the toasty bits over the sage; it will crackle and foam a bit. Let the mixture sit for 1 minute to let the foam subside, then whisk in the olive oil, followed by the red wine vinegar and maple syrup. Season with salt and pepper to taste. Add the cooked sweet potatoes to the pot with the warm lentils. Pour the dressing over the top and stir gently to combine. Add the parsley, season with more salt and pepper, if desired, and toss to combine. Transfer the mixture to a serving dish and sprinkle with goat cheese, if using. Serve warm. Serves four to six.

Wine Pairing: Chardonnay, Grenache, or Merlot.

(Cooking.NewYorkTimes.com, recipe by Yossy Arefi)

Chickpea Pomegranate Salad

INGREDIENTS

    1 cup pomegranate arils
    1 cup chickpeas
    ½ cup seeded diced cucumber
    ½ cup diced red onion
    2 tbsp chopped cilantro (or flat leaf parsley)
    2 tbsp olive oil
    1 tbsp lemon juice
    Salt and pepper to taste

Mix all ingredients in a large bowl. Let rest at room temperature for approx. 30 mins and serve. Serves four.

Wine Pairing: Citrusy Sauvignon Blanc, Viognier, Dry Rose.

Charoset Salad

INGREDIENTS

    For Dressing:
    1/2 cup sweet red wine
    1/2 cup aged balsamic vinegar
    3/4 cup avocado oil
    2 tbsp sugar

1 tsp salt
1/4 tsp cinnamon

For Salad (toss together):
6 oz fresh baby spinach and/or spring mix
3 medium tart apples (such as Gala, Fuji, or Granny Smith) peeled, cored, and coarsely diced
8 dried, pitted dates diced
1 cup candied almonds of walnuts

Combine all dressing ingredients in a jar or container and shake well. The dressing can be made in advance and refrigerated—shake before using. Drizzle over tossed salad just before serving. Serves eight.

Wine Pairing: Chardonnay (unoaked), Riesling, Gewürztraminer.

Cantaloupe Melon Salad with Cucumber and Feta

INGREDIENTS

2 cups cantaloupe melon, cut into chunks (or spooned into balls)
2 cups English cucumber, chopped
1/2 cup crumbled feta cheese
Approx. 15 large fresh mint leaves, chopped

2 tbsp olive oil

1 lime, juiced

Salt and pepper, to taste

Toss everything together in a large bowl, add salt and pepper to taste. Chill for 30 minutes before serving. Serves four.

Wine Pairing: Chenin Blanc, Vouvray (demi-sec), or Prosecco (Italian sparkling).

Barley Roasted Mediterranean Vegetables

INGREDIENTS

1 cup dry pearl barley, washed

2 whole zucchini squash, diced

1 red bell pepper, cored, diced

1 medium/small eggplant, diced

1 medium red onion, diced

1 - 14 oz jar artichoke hearts (packed in water) well drained

Salt and pepper

2 tsp harissa spice, divided (can substitute chili powder)

3/4 tsp smoked paprika, divided

Extra virgin olive oil

2 scallions (green onions), trimmed and chopped (both whites and greens)

1 garlic clove, minced

2 oz chopped fresh parsley

2 tbsp fresh squeezed lemon juice

Feta cheese, to taste

Toasted pine nuts, to taste

Preheat the oven to 425 degrees F. Cook the pearl barley according to the package—this takes 30-45 minutes. While barley is cooking, place all vegetables (zucchini, bell peppers, eggplant, artichoke hearts, and onion) in a large bowl and season with salt, pepper, 1 1/2 tsp harissa spice, and 1/2 teaspoon smoked paprika. Drizzle with extra virgin olive oil. Toss to coat. Spread evenly in one layer on the baking sheet lined with parchment. Roast in a heated oven for approx. 25-30 minutes.

When barley is ready, drain any excess water. Season with salt, pepper, 1/2 teaspoon harissa spice and 1/4 teaspoon smoked paprika. Toss to combine. Transfer cooked barley to a large mixing bowl. Add roasted veggies. Add chopped scallions, garlic, and fresh parsley. Dress with lemon juice and a good drizzle of extra virgin olive oil. Toss. If you like, top with crumbled feta and toasted pine nuts. Serve warm, at room temperature, or cold. Serves up to six.

Wine Pairing: Dry Riesling, or Spanish Tempranillo.

(Inspired by, TheMediterraneanDish.com, recipe by Suzy Karadsheh)

Mediterranean Roasted Eggplant

INGREDIENTS

    1 large globe eggplant, cut into 1-1/2-inch cubes
    3 tbsp extra virgin olive oil
    1/2 tsp salt
    1/4 tsp black pepper
    1/2 tsp ground cumin
    1/4 tsp ground coriander
    1/8 tsp ground cinnamon
    1/4 tsp dried basil
    1/4 tsp dried oregano
    1/4 tsp garlic powder
    1/8 tsp cardamom (optional)
    4 tbsp tahini
    2-3 tbsp warm water
    Juice of half lemon
    1 tbsp fresh parsley, finely chopped
    3 dates, pitted and finely chopped

Preheat the oven to 450 degrees F. Line a baking sheet with parchment paper.

Trim the stem and base off of the eggplant. Slice it horizontally into 1-1/2-inch thick rounds, then cut the rounds into large cubes. Transfer the eggplant to a large bowl. Drizzle it with the olive oil and mix.

In a small dish, mix together the salt, pepper, cumin, coriander, cinnamon, cardamom, dried basil, dried oregano, and garlic powder. Transfer the eggplant to the prepared baking sheet, spreading it out in a single layer. Sprinkle the seasoning blend generously over the eggplant pieces (you'll likely use all or almost all the seasoning). Use your hands to make sure all sides are coated well. Spread eggplant pieces on the lined baking sheet.

Place the baking sheet in the oven. Roast for 20 minutes, then flip the eggplant (suggestion: use a thin metal spatula to gently stir the pieces and turn them). Return to the oven to roast for another 5-10 minutes or until they're tender and browned on all sides (but not shriveled).

While the eggplant roasts, make the tahini sauce:

In a blender or food processor (or in a bowl with a whisk), combine the tahini with 2 tbsp of warm water, lemon juice and salt to taste. Add more water if the mixture is too thick.

Transfer the roasted eggplant to a serving dish. Drizzle it with the tahini sauce (or serve it on the side if you expect to have any leftovers). Top with fresh parsley and the chopped dates.

NOTES:

One large eggplant cut into large cubes should fit onto one large baking sheet. Make sure the cubes are in a single layer and not too close together, otherwise they will steam.

If you do not have dates and would like to add a touch of sweetness to the dish, a small drizzle of honey, date syrup or a few pomegranate seeds are great substitutes. Serves four.

Wine Pairing: Dry Riesling or Viognier, or Italian Reds: Barbera, Primitivo, or Negroamaro.

(StemAndSpoon.com, recipe by Abby Cooper)

Fruited Israeli Couscous

(This warm side dish goes well with Creamy Pheasant Breasts)

INGREDIENTS

    1 tbsp olive oil

    1/4 cup pine nuts

    1/4 cup pistachios

    1/4 cup dried currants (or cranberries)

    1/4 cup chopped dried apricots

    2 tbsp butter

    1/2 medium/large sweet onion very thinly sliced

    2 cups pearl couscous

    2 1/2 cups chicken broth

1/4 cup raisins
1/4 cup Italian parsley, chopped
zest of 1 small lemon1/4-1/2 teaspoon kosher salt adjust to taste

Heat the oil in a large deep skillet over medium heat. Add the pine nuts and pistachios to the skillet. Sauté until toasted and fragrant. Remove from the skillet and set aside. Melt the butter in the skillet and then add the onion and couscous. Cook, while stirring frequently, until browned.

Add the chicken broth, bring to a boil, then reduce to a simmer. Add the dried currents and apricot. Simmer until the couscous is tender, about 6 minutes. Remove from the heat. Add the raisins, toasted nuts, parsley, and lemon zest. Stir to combine. Add salt to taste. And serve warm. Serves six.

Wine Pairing: Chardonnay, Pinot Gris/Pinot Grigio, Chenin Blanc, Viognier, or Sauvignon Blanc.

What Would Jesus Pair?

Apple Matzah Kugel

INGREDIENTS

- 4 matzahs (sheets)
- 3 eggs, beaten
- 1/2 tsp salt
- 1/2 cup brown sugar
- 3 tbsp butter, melted
- 2 tbsp freshly squeezed lemon juice
- 1 1/2 tsp ground cinnamon
- 3 apples - peeled, cored, and cubed
- 1/2 cup raisins (or 1/4 cup raisins and 1/4 cup currents)
- 1/4 tsp ground ginger

Preheat the oven to 350 degrees F. Grease an 8x8 inch baking dish.

Break the matzah sheets into pieces, and soak in a bowl of water until soft. Drain in a colander, pressing to squeeze out the water. In a medium-large bowl, whisk together the eggs, salt, sugar, melted butter, lemon juice, cinnamon, and ginger. Add the soaked matzah and mix well. Fold in the apples and raisins/currants. Spoon into the prepared baking dish and spread evenly.

Bake for 45 minutes in the preheated oven, until browned and the apples are tender. Serves eight.

The Recipes

Wine Pairing: Choose a wine that will pair with the protein course this will accompany.

FISH, POULTRY, AND MEAT

Whole Baked St. Peter's Fish

INGREDIENTS

(The ingredients listed are for one whole tilapia per person and are approximations—this is where you get creative. One whole 8-inch tilapia is about one pound and recommended per person.)

> 1 whole tilapia (or whole branzino, striped bass, black sea bass, flounder, red snapper): ask the fish counter to scale, gut, and thoroughly rinse it.
> Oil with a high smoke point to brush on the fish such as avocado, peanut, canola, or sunflower
> 1 lemon—slice only half of it per person, use the remainder to squeeze on the fish (if not using a sauce)
> Sea salt and freshly ground black pepper
> Garlic powder
> 2 Garlic cloves peeled and sliced in half
> Sprigs of fresh herbs (choose from: dill, thyme, basil, parsley, or cilantro—to go with the sauce you are using)

Optional: Choose from one of the sauces recommended. See recipes that follow.

Preheat the oven to 425 degrees F.

Rinse and pat the fish dry with a paper towel. Transfer it to a foil-lined baking sheet.

Score the fish. If the fish counter did not already do this for you, use a knife to cut slits about an inch apart across the top of the fish. They do not need to be super-deep—just enough to cut through the skin.

Generously brush the outside of the fish on both sides and also inside the slits you just cut with oil. Then brush some oil on the inner cavity of the fish. Generously season the fish inside and out with sea salt, freshly cracked black pepper, and garlic powder to the outside of the fish.

Stuff the cavity with your aromatics: fresh herbs, lemon slices, and garlic. Do experiment with whatever seasonings you prefer. Also, be sure to stuff the garlic all the way into the cavity of the fish because it may burn if it is left exposed.

Place in the preheated oven for 18-20 minutes, or until it reaches an internal temperature of 145 degrees F and flakes easily with a fork. Then remove from the oven. Squeeze the juice from the remaining half of the lemon evenly on top of your baked whole fish if not using a sauce. Serve immediately. Serves one.

Wine Pairing: If serving without sauce: Sauvignon Blanc, Pinot Grigio, Viognier (or white Rhône blend), Soft Chardonnay.

Lemon Cream Sauce

(If using this sauce, then use dill sprigs in your fish along with the lemon and omit the garlic).

INGREDIENTS

    3/4 cup dry white wine

    3 tbsp shallot, minced

    2 tbsp lemon juice, fresh squeezed

    1/2 cup unsalted butter, cut into 6 pieces

    1 1/2 tbsp fresh dill, chopped

    Salt and pepper, to taste

Blend the wine, minced shallot, and lemon juice in a small saucepan and boil approx. 6 minutes over a medium-high flame until reduced to 1/4 cup. Reduce heat to low and add butter, one piece at a time, whisking until melted before adding more. Remove the pan from heat. Stir in the dill. Season to taste with salt and pepper. Serves four.

Wine Pairing: Viognier (or white Rhône blend), Chardonnay, Albariño.

Green Goddess Sauce

(If you don't like cilantro, you can swap it out for extra parsley, dill, mint, or fresh basil. Also, if you're not a fan of heat, you can leave out the jalapeno).

INGREDIENTS

- 1/2 bunch cilantro
- 1/2 bunch parsley
- 1 cup Greek yogurt
- 2 scallions (green onions), sliced
- 2 cloves garlic, peeled and smashed
- 1 lime, juiced
- 1 jalapeño, seeded and diced (optional)
- 1/4 cup olive oil
- 1 tbsp white wine vinegar
- Salt and pepper, to taste

Place all ingredients in a food processor or blender and process until desired texture is reached. Season with salt and pepper, to taste. Serves eight.

Wine Pairing: Sauvignon Blanc (from Chile or New Zealand), Verdejo (Spanish).

Greek Ladolemono Sauce

INGREDIENTS

    1/4 cup fresh lemon juice (juice of 2 large lemons)
    1 to 2 tsp dried oregano
    1 large garlic clove minced
    3/4 tsp kosher salt
    3/4 tsp black pepper
    3/4 cup extra virgin olive oil

Add all ingredients except olive oil in a bowl and whisk to combine. While you are whisking vigorously, slowly drizzle in the extra virgin olive oil. Serves two.

Wine Pairing: Whites from Greece, Dry Whites: Sauvignon Blanc, Pinot Grigio, Viognier (or white Rhône blend), Soft Chardonnay.

Romesco Sauce

    (Spanish roasted red pepper sauce)

INGREDIENTS

    1 16-ounce jar roasted red peppers, drained
    2 thick slices baguette, lightly toasted
    3 Roma tomatoes, quartered
    1/2 cup almonds, raw or roasted
    2 tbsp flat-leaf parsley, chopped

2 tbsp Sherry vinegar (or red wine vinegar)
1 tsp smoked paprika
1/2 tsp cayenne pepper
1 1/2 tsp salt
3 cloves garlic, peeled and smashed
1/4 cup extra virgin olive oil
Salt and pepper, to taste

Place the first eight ingredients in a food processor and blend until finely chopped. While still running, drizzle in olive oil and blend until smooth. Season with salt and pepper, to taste. Serves eight.

Wine Pairing: Pinot Noir, Garnacha (Spanish Grenache), Merlot (cool-climate/France or Italy), Beaujolais.

Mediterranean Fish Stew

INGREDIENTS
   1 tbsp olive oil
   1 onion, diced
   4 cloves of garlic, minced
   1 bulb of fennel, diced
   1 red pepper, chopped

1 cup dry white wine

1 28-ounce can of diced tomatoes, with juices (or 4-5 whole tomatoes)

1 tsp red pepper flakes

1 tsp dried oregano

1 pound halibut, cod, or other firm white fish

1/2 cup chopped fresh herbs (suggested: combination of oregano, rosemary, basil, and chives)

1/2 cup crumbled feta

Heat the olive oil in a large heavy-bottomed pot or Dutch oven over medium heat. Sauté the onion until soft, about 6 minutes. Add the garlic and sauté an additional minute. Add in the fennel and red peppers and continue to cook until just soft.

Pour in the white wine and simmer for several minutes, until reduced by about half.

Stir in the tomatoes, oregano, and red pepper flakes. Cover and simmer for 15-20 minutes. Season to taste with salt and pepper. Add an additional half cup of water if necessary, depending on how much liquid simmered off.

Cut the fish into bite-sized pieces and add the fish. Continue to simmer until fish is cooked through, about 5 minutes.

Remove from the heat and stir in the fresh herbs. Ladle the soup into bowls and top with fresh feta. Serves four.

Wine Pairing: Beaujolais, Gamay (French from Beaujolais), Pinot Noir, Dry Riesling.

(BunsenBurnerBakery.com)

Mediterranean Spiced Game Hens

INGREDIENTS
2 celery sticks, cleaned and chopped in large pieces
1 large sweet onion, roughly chopped
1 lime or lemon, juiced
4 Cornish hens, roughly 1 pound to 1 1/2 pounds each
2 cup chicken broth

For the Garlic and Spice Marinade:
15-20 garlic cloves
Salt
2 1/2 tsp hot or sweet paprika
1 1/2 tsp ground allspice
1 1/2 tsp dried thyme
1 tsp ground black pepper
1/2 tsp nutmeg
1 lemon or lime, juiced
2 tbsp extra virgin olive oil

Preheat the oven to 425 degrees F. Make the Mediterranean garlic and spice marinade. Combine the garlic spice rub ingredients in the food processor. Run the processor until you achieve a pasty spice mixture or rub.

Now to each of the hens, apply the marinade generously on the outside and in the cavities. Lift the skins and apply some of the marinade underneath (this is the key to flavor).

Heat a lightly oiled cast iron grill or skillet. Turn the heat to medium-high and brown each of the hens on all sides. Set the hens aside momentarily to cool.

Once the hens are cool enough to handle, stuff each hen's cavity with the chopped onions and celery. Now squeeze juice of one lime or lemon on the hens. Add all the used lime or lemon halves in with the onion and celery stuffing. Sprinkle each hen lightly with a dash of seasoned salt, if you like.

Place the hens in a large cast iron skillet or a roasting pan. Add two cups of quality chicken broth to the side of the skillet. Bake in the 425 degrees F heated oven for 1 hour to 1 hour and 15 minutes or until the hen juices run clean, basting every 15 minutes with the broth. Remove from the oven and cover loosely with foil for 15 minutes before serving. Serves four to six depending on the size of the hens.

Wine Pairing: Chardonnay, Semillon (from Bordeaux), Viognier and Gewürztraminer (if using hot paprika).

The Recipes

(TheMediterraneanDish.com, recipe by Suzy Karadsheh)

Roasted Chicken with Lemon and Thyme

INGREDIENTS

    3/4 stick plus 1 tbsp unsalted butter, softened

    2 tbsp fresh thyme leaves

    4 tbsp fresh lemon juice

    1/3 cup dry white wine

    Kosher salt

    Freshly ground black pepper

    1 (5-pound) whole chicken, patted dry

    1 medium yellow onion peeled and quartered

    1 lemon, quartered

Preheat the oven to 425 degrees F. In a small bowl, blend the 3/4 stick of softened butter with the thyme leaves, 3 tbsp of the lemon juice, and salt and pepper.

Fill the cavity of the chicken with the lemon and onion quarters. Rub the lemon-thyme butter mixture all over the chicken and season with salt and pepper. You may tie the chicken legs together with kitchen twine for a nicer presentation. Place the prepared chicken in a large Dutch oven pot, breast side up. Tuck in wings under the chicken or clip the wing tips to prevent them from burning. Add 1/3 cup of white wine to the bottom of the pot.

Cover and roast in a preheated oven for 1 hour 15 minutes. Remove the lid and roast for an additional 30 minutes—or until an instant-read thermometer inserted in the inner thigh reaches 160°F. Transfer the chicken to a carving board and let rest for 10-15 minutes.

Meanwhile, skim off all but 1 tbsp of fat from the pan juices. Stir in the remaining 1 tbsp of lemon juice and cook over moderate heat until hot, 1 to 2 minutes. Remove from the heat and stir in the remaining 1 tbsp of butter. Season with salt and pepper.

Carve the chicken and transfer to a platter. Spoon the pan sauce on top and serve. Serves four.

Wine Pairing: Soft Chardonnay (not oaky), White Rhônes such as Viognier and Grenache Blanc, or Citrusy Sauvignon Blanc.

Creamy Pheasant Breasts

(This recipe works well with chicken breasts and goes well with Fruited Israeli Couscous)

INGREDIENTS
    6 skinless, boneless pheasant breast halves
    salt and black pepper to taste
    1 medium shallot, finely chopped

1/2 cup all-purpose flour
1 tsp garlic powder
1/4 cup butter
1/4 cup avocado, safflower, or any light oil
1/2 cup dry white wine
1/3 cup chicken broth or stock
1 1/2 cup heavy cream

Preheat an oven to 325 degrees F. Season the pheasant breasts on all sides with salt and pepper. In a shallow bowl, mix garlic powder and salt and pepper with the flour. Dredge the pheasant breast with the flour mixture until completely coated. Shake off excess flour and set aside. Melt the butter and olive oil in a Dutch oven pot over medium heat. Add the pheasant breasts and brown until golden brown on both sides, about 5 minutes per side.

Remove pheasant breasts from the pot and set aside. Over a medium flame, add shallots and stir for 1 minute, then white wine and deglaze the pan stirring for 1 minute. Add the chicken broth stirring to a simmer and slowly add the heavy cream. Bring to a simmer again and add the pheasant breasts coating them with the cream sauce. Cover and bake for an hour. The breasts should be tender and no longer pink in the center. Serves six.

Wine Pairing: Chardonnay, Pinot Gris/Pinot Grigio, Chenin Blanc, Viognier, Sauvignon Blanc.

What Would Jesus Pair?

Passover Beef Brisket

INGREDIENTS

1-5 pound brisket

8 garlic cloves cut lengthwise into 4 pieces

Sea salt

4 cups beef stock

2 sweet onions thinly sliced

1 cup chili sauce

1/4 cup brown sugar

1 tsp paprika

1 tsp smoked paprika

1 tsp dried thyme

2 bay leaves

Preheat the oven to 500 degrees F. Place the brisket on a work surface. If necessary, trim the fat cap to an even 1/4-inch layer.

Using a paring knife, make small incisions in the meat and shove a piece of garlic into each. Do this until the meat is stuffed with garlic all over. Season both sides with salt and pepper and place the brisket in a large Dutch oven or rimmed baking dish/roasting pan (preferably metal) starting with the fat cap facing up and brown it in the oven, about 10 minutes per side.

Remove the pan from the oven and pour in the beef stock (NOTE: if you are using a Pyrex dish, wait a few minutes for the pan to acclimate to room temperature so it does not shatter.). Turn the oven down to 350 degrees, cover the dish with a lid or foil, and cook in the oven for 1 hour.

In the meantime, heat 1 tbsp of olive oil over medium-low heat in a large skillet. Add the onions and sauté, stirring every until soft and caramelized. Remove the meat from the oven, and add the chili sauce, brown sugar, paprika, smoked paprika, cayenne, thyme, and bay leaves to the pan. Whisk everything together with the beef stock. Arrange the caramelized onions on top of the meat. Cover the pan again with the lid or foil and return it to the oven for 2-3 hours. NOTE: if you want to be able to cut the brisket into slices, take it out at 2 hours. If you want it to be falling apart, keep it in for the full 3 hours.

Remove the meat from the oven and transfer it to a cutting board. Slice the brisket against the grain into slices. Return the meat to the sauce and serve. Serves ten.

Wine Pairing: Sangiovese, Chianti (DOCG), Syrah/Shiraz, or Carménère (a medium bodied red from Chile).

(FeedMePhoebe.com, recipe by Phoebe Lapine)

Lamb with Figs and Red Wine

INGREDIENTS

    2 large sweet onions, chopped

    4 cloves garlic, minced

    3 tbsp olive oil

    3 lb boneless leg of lamb, cubed

    1 cup beef stock

    1 1/2 cups dry red wine

    1/4 cup aged balsamic

    2 bay leaves

    2 tsp dried mustard

    2 tsp dried coriander

    2 tsp ground cumin

    1/2 tsp cinnamon

    1/4 tsp ground ginger

    1/4 tsp cayenne pepper

    1/2 tsp salt

    1 cup dried figs, cut into quarters

    1 tbsp brown sugar

    Cooked rice (serve on a bed of cooked rice)

Preheat an oven to 325 degrees F. Add olive oil to a Dutch oven and heat over a medium-high flame, add the lamb, onions, and garlic and braise until the meat is well seared, and the onion and garlic begin to brown, be careful that the mixture doesn't burn. Stir in beef stock, wine, vinegar, bay leaves, dried spices, and salt, bring to a boil. Place the cover on the Dutch oven and bake in a preheated oven for 1 hour 45 minutes.

Remove from the oven and stir in the quartered figs and brown sugar. Replace the lid and return to the oven for an additional 20 minutes until the lamb is tender. Serve over rice. Serves eight to ten.

Wine Pairing: Grenache, Syrah, Tempranillo, Negroamaro (Italy).

(Inspired by *Cooking with the Bible—Recipes for Biblical Meal* by Anthony Chiffolo and Rayner Hesse, Greenwood Press 2006, page 87)

DESSERTS

Red Wine Poached Pears

INGREDIENTS

    3 cups red wine, (Cabernet, Merlot, Zinfandel, or your favorite dry red wine)
    1/3 cup plus 1 tbsp sugar
    3/4 cup apple cider, orange juice, or pomegranate juice
    3/4 cup raspberries
    1 large strip fresh orange zest
    2 cinnamon stick
    3 cloves
    2 star anise (optional)
    3 tsp vanilla
    6 firm, ripe pears (Bosc, Anjou, or Asian - do not use Bartletts)
    One 8 oz container mascarpone cheese
    Orange zest for garnish

Carefully peel pears, leaving the stems intact. Slice 1/4 to 1/2 inch off the bottom and set aside. In a large saucepan (make sure you can fit 6 pears upright, so they don't fall over), combine all ingredients except for the pears. Bring the liquid to a boil, reduce heat and simmer for 5-7 minutes.

Gently place pears in poaching liquid, cover, and simmer for 20-30 minutes. Turn the pears carefully to ensure even color every 5 minutes, until the pears are cooked and still firm. Remove saucepan from stove, uncover and let cool. When completely cooled, cover and chill in the refrigerator for at least 3 hours. They can be refrigerated for up to 24 hours (if you do this it's a good idea to turn them occasionally). Gently remove pears from liquid and allow them to come to room temperature.

Meanwhile, reduce liquid by about half over a medium-high heat for about 15-20 minutes. The liquid should become slightly syrupy. Remove from the stove and let liquid come to room temperature.

Drizzle each pear with 2 tbsp syrup and serve with a generous dollop of mascarpone and a grating of orange zest. Serves six.

Wine Pairing: Ruby Port, or Côtes du Rhône.

Honey Almond Cake

(Almonds, honey, and rose water come together to give a lovely Middle Eastern touch)

INGREDIENTS

    1 1/2 cup all purpose flour

    1 1/4 tsp baking powder

    1/2 tsp baking soda

1/4 tsp salt

1/4 cup almond meal (almond flour)

1/4 cup raw sugar (or regular white sugar)

3/4 cup coconut yogurt (or plain Greek yogurt)

1/3 cup coconut oil (or any vegetable oil)

1/4 cup plus 1 tbsp honey

4-5 drops almond extract

1/2 tsp rose water

1/4 cup slivered almonds

For Honey Syrup:

1 1/2 tbsp water

1 1/2 tbsp honey

4-5 drops rose water

Preheat the oven to 350 degrees F. Grease a 6-inch cake pan.

Sift the flour, baking powder, baking soda, and salt in a bowl. Add almond meal/flour and raw sugar to the dry ingredients. In another bowl, whisk together honey, yogurt, coconut oil, almond extract, and rose water. Pour over the dry ingredients and gently mix. Do not over mix. Pour into the prepared pan. Smoothen the surface and sprinkle slivered almonds. Bake for 30-35 minutes or until a skewer inserted in the center comes out clean. Let the cake cool in the pan for 5-10 minutes before turning it out on a cooling rack.

In the meantime, make the honey syrup:

Bring the water to a boil. Take it off the heat, stir in honey and rose water. Let the syrup cool.

Once the cake is ready, use a skewer to poke holes all over the top of the warm cake. Spoon over the cooled honey syrup. Let the syrup soak in for 30 minutes or so. Garnish with dried rose petals and serve at room temperature. Serves eight.

Wine Pairing: Demi-sec Champagne, Almond Sparling, Sweet Riesling.

(TashasArtisanFoods.com/blog, recipe by Natasha Minocha)

Flourless Chocolate Cake

INGREDIENTS

    6 tbsp unsalted butter, plus a little extra for pan

    8 oz fine quality semi-sweet chocolate (not unsweetened), chopped into small pieces

    1/2 cup granulated sugar

    6 large eggs

    Unsweetened cocoa powder or confectioners' sugar for dusting

    Whipped cream and raspberries for topping, if desired

Preheat the oven to 275 degrees F with the rack in the middle of the oven.

Butter the bottom and sides of a 9-inch springform pan. Line the bottom with a round of wax or parchment paper and butter the paper. Place chocolate and butter in a large microwave safe bowl and microwave in 30-second increments, stirring each time, until completely melted. Whisk in sugar, let cool for at least 5 minutes (so that the eggs don't curdle), and whisk in eggs. Pour batter into the buttered and papered pan and smooth the top with a rubber spatula.

Bake for 45-50 minutes, until the cake has formed a thin crust and pulls away from the sides of the pan. Test with a toothpick that comes out with a few crumbs, but not gooey.

Cool completely on a wire rack and then remove sides of the pan. Dust cake with unsweetened cocoa powder or confectioners' sugar. Serve with whipped cream and raspberries, if desired. Serves eight.

Wine Pairing: California Cabernet Sauvignon or Sauternes from Bordeaux (sweet white).

(CaWineClub.com)

The Recipes

Song of Songs Nut Cakes

(This is an ancient Egyptian recipe from 1600 BC, discovered on an ostracon—piece of pottery)

INGREDIENTS
1 cup fresh or juicy dried pitted dates or figs
1/4 - 1/2 cup water
1 tsp ground cinnamon
1/4 tsp ground cardamom
1/2 cup chopped walnuts
3/4 cup chopped almonds
Honey

In a food processor, mix the dates and water into a paste. Add the spices, walnuts and 1/4 cup of almonds (reserving the rest to coat) and mix well. Form into small balls, coat with honey, and roll in remaining almonds.

Wine Pairing: Dry Sparkling or pair with the other desserts, or if using with a charcuterie.

24

A Little Bit About the Wines

Armed with a little knowledge of the wines I suggested, you will have more fun deciding which of the wines to pair with your dish.

With over 10,000 grape varietals grown throughout the world, there are countless possibilities for interesting food and wine pairings. The suggestions I have made at the end of the recipes are just that—suggestions—based on my experience and knowledge (and wine that you will readily find locally). They will work based on weight, balance, and flavor among other attributes of both the food and the wine. With that said, please experiment as you feel confident—the brief descriptions below should help you. And always remember to drink what you like; the pairing will not work if you do not like the wine.

While a lot of Mediterranean food goes well with red wine, I have not made many red wine suggestions because of the nature of the recipes presented. I have added descriptions of some of the classic varietals for insight and because I simply love to drink them.

A meal without wine is like a day without sunshine.

Champagne vs Sparkling Wine

Sparkling wine can only be called "Champagne" if it is made in the region of Champagne in France. To clarify, all Champagne is sparkling wine, but not all sparkling wine is Champagne. Prosecco is sparkling wine from Italy, Cava is sparkling wine from Spain (and is generally less acidic than Champagne).

Sparkling wines/Champagne range from Demi-sec which is sweeter, to Brut which is dry, and Extra Brut which is very dry. Pink Champagne or Rosé Champagne is made by one of three methods including mixing red and white wines. Almond Sparkling is sparkling wine with an essence of natural almond added and sometimes on the sweeter side, but yummy. And tiny bubbles are better!

Albariño is a high-quality, light-bodied white that grows mostly in Spain and Portugal. It's loved for its high acidity, refreshing citrus flavors, dry taste, and subtle saltiness. It will impart lemon, lime, grapefruit, and pear flavors, and even a hint of beeswax. With a bit of bottle aging, those delicious fruity flavors develop into sweeter notes of peach and apricot, and sometimes more complex notes of nuts and almonds will appear.

Barbera is primarily a dry, non-sparkling wine that grows mostly in Italy and ranges from medium-bodied to full-bodied with low tannins and high acidity. The most common tasting notes include red fruit, such as sour cherry, strawberry, and raspberry.

A Little Bit About the Wines

Beaujolais is from Beaujolais France and is a medium-bodied red wine that's light on tannins and tends to have a bright, juicy freshness to it, even when it is aged.

Cabernet Sauvignon is one of the world's most widely recognized red wine grape varieties. It is grown in nearly every major wine producing country. It is recognized through its prominence hailing from the Bordeaux region in France. Flavors will vary depending on where the grapes are grown and the specific winemaking process. But in general, Cabernet Sauvignon has dark fruit flavors of blackcurrant (cassis), black cherry, blackberry with notes of green bell pepper, spice, tobacco, wood, and vanilla (from aging in oak barrels).

Cabernet Franc is a French red wine grape that is planted in all major wine-producing regions of the world. It is usually blended with other grapes in Bordeaux-style red wines, but Cabernet Franc is also made as a single-varietal wine in some regions. The flavors are a balance between red fruits, herbs, and peppery earthiness. Cabernet Franc has medium-to-high acidity that makes it refreshingly easy-to-drink.

Carménère is a red wine variety that is quite often full of bold cherry, plum, pepper, and spice. It originated in France, but little is found there today after being almost wiped out by phylloxera. Ninety-eight percent of Carménère is grown in Chile.

Chardonnay is a white grape variety that is widely planted around the world (and would take up an entire chapter in this book). It can be a bit of a chameleon, covering a wide range of styles from crisp and refreshing to velvety or big and bold. It's even one of the main grape varieties that Champagne is made from. Chardonnay naturally has hints of fruit like melons and apples and pears. Chardonnays that have been aged in oak barrels typically have flavors and aromas of cinnamon, clove, and vanilla, and if it's gone through malolactic fermentation, hints of butter are likely to be found. Some Chardonnays are aged in stainless tanks and impart flavors of green apples, lemons, and pineapple.

Chenin Blanc is a white wine grape variety originating from the Loire Valley of France. Its high acidity means it can be used to make varieties from sparkling wines to well-balanced dessert wines. It is medium bodied and is full of floral and honeyed aromas with quince and apple-like flavors. Chenin Blanc is often dry but is made into sweeter styles as well.

Chianti is a red wine blend from Tuscany, Italy, made primarily with Sangiovese grapes (70 percent) and Chianti Classico must contain 80 percent Sangiovese. Common tasting notes include red fruits, dried herbs, balsamic vinegar, smoke, and game. I can also show notes of preserved sour cherries, dried oregano, balsamic reduction, espresso, and sweet tobacco. It is ruby red in color with flashes of bright burnt orange. Great with Italian dishes and especially pizza.

Côtes du Rhône is a wine of the Rhône region. It can be red, white, and rosé wine, produced from Grenache for reds and rosés, or Grenache Blanc for white wine. Whites are traditionally Grenache Blanc with Viognier and Clairette, which create floral-scented, full-bodied wines with peach, lemon, and honey notes. In a typical Côtes du Rhône red, you'll have a mix of Grenache, Syrah, and Mourvèdre, plus Cinsault and Carignan. It is an easy-drinking, full-bodied wine, featuring flavors of black currant, plum, and spice, with approachable tannins and a lengthy finish.

Fumé Blanc—Fumé is French for "smoky", Blanc is French for "white" and Blanc Fumé is the name given to Sauvignon Blanc produced in the regions of Sancerre and Pouilly-Fumé in the Loire Valley of France. It has a natural "smoky" character (which is not due to oak barrel fermentation). Fumé Blanc is the American name for Sauvignon Blanc made with an oak influence to emulate the characteristics of Blanc Fumé.

Gamay is a light-bodied red wine that's similar in taste to Pinot Noir. In fact, this variety is a cousin of Pinot Noir, and it grows primarily next to Burgundy, France, in a region called Beaujolais. Gamay wines are loved for their delicate floral aromas, subtle earthy notes, and surprising ability to pair with food (even fish).

Gewürztraminer (ga-VERTZ-trah-mee-ner) is a white wine grape originating in the Alsace region of France. It is a classic grape that likes cool climates like northeast France, Germany, and northern Italy, and is used to make a white wine of the same name. The predominant nose and flavor is lychee—a sweet, tropical fruit. It is higher in alcohol than comparable white wines. While not as well-known as Chardonnay and Pinot Grigio, it is typically very affordable and pairs well with spicy, flavorful foods.

Grenache vs Garnacha are the same grape variety. The difference is that Grenache is the typical French name of the grape while Garnacha is the more common name in Spain. There are many styles of this wine from light to big, robust wines. Some consider the lighter style of Grenache to be very much like Pinot Noir. Spice and red fruit, as in cherry, raspberry, and strawberry, can be identified in a Grenache wine. Grenache can also be a more robust style.

Grenache Blanc is a variety of white wine grape that is related to the red grape Grenache. It is mostly found in Rhône wine blends and in northeast Spain. Its wines are characterized by high alcohol and low acidity, with citrus and or herbaceous notes. It is a delightful wine and often blended with Viognier and Picpoul Blanc.

Grüner Veltliner is a white wine grape variety grown primarily in Austria. It is a dry white wine with flavors of green pepper and lime and is an exotic alternative to Sauvignon Blanc.

A Little Bit About the Wines

Malbec is a full-bodied red wine that grows mostly in Argentina. Known for its plump, dark fruit flavors and smoky finish, Malbec wine offers a great alternative to higher-priced Cabernet Sauvignon and Syrah.

Mourvèdre is a meaty and full-bodied red wine. Its aroma is an explosion of dark fruit, flowers like violet and herbaceous aroma of black pepper, thyme, and red meat. In regions such as Bandol, France, and Jumilla, Spain, Mourvèdre wine can have a very gamey taste.

Merlot is a juicy, elegant, and versatile red grape variety that's grown around the globe, but it's world famous for its role in the luxurious blends of Bordeaux. While Merlot's characteristics vary depending on the climate, soil, and winemaking techniques, wines made with the grape are typically dry and can show flavors of red and black fruits, softer tannins, and medium to medium-high body and acidity.

Montepulciano is a dark red wine made from the varietal of the same name. Hailing from the Tuscan hilltop town of Montepulciano, this thick-skinned red grape is a cousin of the Sangiovese grape and is mostly grown in central Italy. This grape is robust and versatile, it often produces deeply colored and extract-rich wines. Despite its thick skin, the grape's high juice-to-skin ratio ensures wines of modest tannin levels.

Nebbiolo is known as the "King" of red wine in Italy. This variety is big, bold, and high in everything (acid, alcohol, and tannin). Despite being a robust wine, its color is lighter red with soft shades of garnet and orange. Nebbiolo has many aromas and flavors. Most can be described as earthy or rustic. Red berries, roses, herbs, and licorice are some of the key aromas and flavors in this powerful wine.

Negroamaro is a red grape that is native to Southern Italy and grows in abundance in Puglia, but almost nowhere else. It produces earthy wines with rich black fruit flavors—mainly, prunes and ripe plum, blackberry, and sweet cherries—with a faint herbaceous finish reminiscent of dried thyme or sharp, aromatic spices like allspice or clove. It's fairly dry on the palate, because of its relatively high tannins, but ultimately a full-bodied grape.

Petite Sirah is often confused with Syrah. They are related, but not the same grape. And there's really nothing "petite" about it. The grapes produce an inky color and rich, deep flavor—mostly fruity, and is certainly complex. It will have flavors of blackberry, blueberry, and plum. You will also notice tastes of chocolate or cocoa, as well as black pepper and other earthy elements.

Pinot Gris vs Pinot Grigio: Though the two wines share identical origin, they are very different. Pinot Gris and Pinot Grigio wines are categorized based on whether they're made in the French or the Italian style. Pinot Grigio, undoubtedly the most popular of the two, is lighter-bodied, crisp, clean, and vibrant with citrus flavors.

Pinot Gris, on the other hand, is sweet, and has spicy tropical fruit aromas. It generally has low acidity, higher alcohol levels, and a rich texture.

Pinot Blanc is a white wine grape used to make a dry French wine. The grapes can be used to make still, sparkling, and sweet dessert wines, and is often compared to Chardonnay because of its high acidity and it is dry with a medium to full body, and bright flavor. Depending on how it is made, Pinot Blanc can be light and refreshing, or oaked and full-bodied. This wine has a strong fragrance with notes of apple and almond and is medium to high in alcohol content.

Pinot Noir is a red wine grape now dominant in Burgundy, France, and popular around the world. At first glance, these wines are mostly pale to medium in color due to their thin skins but have a unique profile of aromas and flavor. Its aroma imparts cherries, red berries and stewed fruit and is often accompanied by earthiness, spice, and, when oak-aged, gentle wafts of vanilla and smoke. This beautiful wine also has a complex array of flavors, from ripe cherry and raspberry to the earthiness of forest floor, tea leaves, and sometimes even clove.

Primitivo is an Italian red grape (originally from Croatia) that produces bold wines with smooth flavors of blackberry, dark chocolate and licorice. It produces jam-like fruit-forward wine bursting with blackberry, black plum, strawberry, sweet cooking spice, licorice, vanilla, and tobacco. Primitivo can be dry to sweet, is medium to full-bodied, has medium to high tannins, low to medium acidity, and has high alcohol.

Riesling is a white grape variety that originated in the Rhine region of Germany. It is an aromatic grape with flowery, almost perfumed, aromas as well as high acidity. It is used to make dry, semi-sweet, sweet, and sparkling white wines. Riesling wines are usually varietally pure and are seldom oaked.

Rosé is a type of wine that incorporates some of the color from the grape skins, but not enough to qualify it as a red wine. While it's produced similarly to other red wines, the time it ferments with grape skins is cut shorter. This reduced skin contact is what gives Rosé its signature pink color. The flavors lean on the fruity side, so you can expect hints of strawberry, citrus, melon, raspberry, cherry, and fresh flowers. Even though Rosé wines tend to the lighter side, they still offer a lovely range of sweet to savory to dry. Of course, depending on the type of grape the Rosé wine is made with, the flavor will greatly vary. The Provence wine region of France creates Rosé more than any other style of wine—and they are simply delightful.

Sauternes is a French sweet wine from the region of the same name in the Graves section in Bordeaux. Sauternes wine is made from Sémillon, Sauvignon Blanc, and Muscadelle grapes that have been affected by Botrytis cinerea, also known as noble rot. This causes the grapes to become partially raisin, resulting in concentrated and distinctively flavored wines. Sauternes are characterized by the balance of sweetness with the zest of acidity. Some common flavor notes include apricots, honey, peaches but with a nutty note. It lingers on the palate with a long finish.

Sangiovese is Italy's most widely planted red grape variety, it is used to make a variety of wines, including Chianti. It is a dry, light to medium-bodied red wine that tips towards higher levels of mouth-watering acidity and tighter tannins. The rich flavors range from rustic to fruity, depending on where and how the vines are managed. For fruit, expect cherry, plum, and red currant, as well as smoky and earthy herbaceousness.

Sauvignon Blanc is a green-skinned grape variety that originates from the city of Bordeaux in France. Its taste is very different from other white wines, like Chardonnay, because of its green and herbaceous flavors. The primary fruit flavors of Sauvignon Blanc are lime, green apple, passion fruit, and white peach. Depending on how ripe the grapes are when the wine is made, the flavor will range from zesty lime to flowery peach. New Zealand's cool and maritime climate, combined with its diverse soil types and winemaking techniques, contribute to the distinctiveness of their Sauvignon Blanc.

Sémillon is a golden-skinned grape used to make dry and sweet white wines, primarily in France and Australia. It's most frequently associated with the white wines of

Bordeaux, where it is generally blended with Sauvignon Blanc and Muscadelle. Many of the great sweet (dessert) wines of Sauternes also rely on Sémillon as part of their blend.

Silvaner is an underrated, neutral-scented, white-wine grape used widely in western Germany, and just across the Rhine in Alsace where it is spelled Sylvaner. Silvaner is typically medium-bodied and has mild acidity, with earthy and mineral tones that underscore fruity notes of honeydew melon and orchard fruit and herbal or vegetal notes reminiscent of celery or fresh-cut grass.

Shiraz vs Syrah: They both refer to the same grape; Syrah is how the variety was originally referred to while Shiraz is how it became known in Australia. Syrah, mostly referring to Old World style, is lighter in body and alcohol, leaner and with finer tannins. Shiraz, on the other hand, refers to New World, intense wines, which are generally richer, with riper aromas and fuller in both body and alcohol. It has a range of flavors, from smoke, bacon, herbs, red and black fruits, white and black pepper, to floral violet notes. When aged in oak, Syrah takes on flavors of vanilla and baking spice. In general, Syrah will be more elegant, lean, and savory than its powerful, fruit-driven cousin Shiraz.

Tempranillo is a black grape variety widely grown to make full-bodied red wines in its native Spain and the main grape of the region of Rioja. The most dominant flavors often include cherry, dried fig, cedar, and tobacco. Age impacts the flavors of Tempranillo, imparting juicy fruit flavors and heat. Really beautiful vintages feature deeper, darker fruit notes, dry leaves, and Tempranillo's signature leather flavors.

Verdejo is an uncommon, light-bodied white wine that grows almost exclusively in Spain. The wine is an outstanding alternative to Sauvignon Blanc and Pinot Grigio. Verdejo produces subtle, refreshing white wines with flavors of lime, grapefruit, grass, fennel, and almonds. Similar to Sauvignon Blanc, it has high acidity and some green flavors, but takes on a richer, nuttier feel when aged, either in bottle or barrel.

Vermentino was originally thought to have come from Spain, but it has been established that the grape actually comes from Italy (where it is still widely planted). Typical aromas include lime, grapefruit, though aromas can become more tropical such as pineapple and mango in warmer climates. This wine enjoys medium to low sweetness, medium body and good acidity. Sometimes a hint of saltiness comes through as it is often planted near the sea.

Viognier is a full-bodied white wine that hails from the Rhône region of Southern France. Most loved for its complex nose unrivaled by other white wines, it's bursting with natural aromas of peaches and apricots alongside the floral scents of honeysuckle and violets and a hint of almond or allspice. This exotic variety is generally golden in color, dry, and can be oaked or unoaked. Viognier blends well with Chenin Blanc, and Grenache Blanc. Hands down this is one of my favorite wines (and the first Estate wine bottled by our winery, Sharp's Hill Vineyards).

Vouvray is a white wine made with Chenin Blanc grapes that grow along the banks of the Loire River in France. The wines range in style from dry to sweet, and still to sparkling, each with its own distinct character. It is famous for being demi-sec or off-dry wine, which means it is half-sweet wine that helps to balance the acidity and vital minerals. Regardless of style, Vouvray is loved for its delicate floral aromas while bursting with flavors of pear, honeysuckle, quince, and apple.

Zinfandel is a red wine grape variety that is the second most planted red grape in California. The dark blue Zinfandel grape can be used to make bold red wine with high tannins and medium acidity or "White Zin," a pink, affordable wine. While made from the same grapes, the two wines are distinctively different in flavor, body, sweetness, alcohol content, and price. Red Zin has lots of jam-like, fruity flavor of raspberry, blackberry, cherry, plums, cinnamon, black pepper, and licorice all wrapped around various intensities of oak, and is high in alcohol. Conversely, White Zin has a light, sweet flavor and low alcohol.